Clever Cooking
for One or Two

Fabulous recipes ❀ Simple to prepare ❀ No waste

DAIRY COOKBOOK

Executive Editor	Nick Rowe
Managing Editor	Emily Anderson
Editor	Emma Callery
Designer	Graham Meigh
Proof Reader	Aune Butt
Indexer	Christine Bernstein
Photographer	Steve Lee
Food Stylist	Sara Lewis
Props Stylist	Jo Harris
Recipes created by	Pat Alburey
	Kathryn Hawkins
	Lucy Knox
	Sue McMahon
	Kate Moseley
Nutritional consultant	Dr Wendy Doyle
Recipe testers	Iain Anderson
	Carolyn Glazebrook
	Katy Hackforth
	Claire Nadin
	Chris Perry
	Kate Timmins
Production	Priti Kothary
	Teresa Wellborne

Eaglemoss Consumer Publications Ltd
Electra House, Electra Way, Crewe, Cheshire, CW1 6WZ
Telephone 01270 270050 Website www.dairydiary.co.uk

First printed March 2008
© Eaglemoss Consumer Publications Ltd
ISBN-13: 978-0-9554232-4-6
123456789

Contents

Cooking and shopping for one or two

You are not alone if you live alone, or with just one other person. In Britain, at least 65 per cent of all households are occupied by one or two people with the majority of homes in the UK catering for singles or small families. Of course, many larger families have fragmented meal times and children eat separately. So, there is a real demand for good quality recipes written for just one or two people.

For many of us, cooking in small quantities can be a real chore and most recipes seem to cater for at least four people. However, this book is different; the chapters include recipes for one person (easily doubled for two) as well as a choice of recipes for two people.

For busy, single people or couples, it is often easier to grab ready-meals, frozen foods or packet mixes from the supermarket. These foods, however, are often loaded with additives, fat, salt and sugar. Home-cooked food is created by you, so you know exactly what has gone into it. You can use good, fresh ingredients and ensure you are getting a really good balanced diet. Therefore, it really is worth making the effort to cook your own food from scratch, and it's often easier than you think – especially using the recipes in this book. All the recipes are simple to prepare, have plenty of tips to help you, and give the calories and fat per portion, so you know exactly what you are eating.

One of the frustrations of cooking for fewer people is wasting food. No one likes to throw away food, but it can be hard to avoid this in a small household. So, each recipe in this book only uses fresh ingredients that you can buy in just the quantity you need, plus a few storecupboard standbys (see box) that should last for at least a few weeks. It really does help you to cook and shop easily and economically, but eat very well. So, give your tastebuds a treat and give some of these delicious recipes a try – as well as being kind to your conscience and to your purse!

Shop 'til you chop

Shopping for one or two is in some ways more challenging than the cooking. Follow these tips to minimise wastage.

- Plan meals in advance, so that you only buy what you need.
- Write a list and stick to it.
- Keep a list of what you have in stock that needs eating up.
- Buy meat from the butcher or supermarket meat counter so you can ask for just what you need.
- If you buy larger packs, freeze individual portions in bags the same day as you buy them.
- Check use-by dates when you buy.
- Visit local shops and farmers' markets rather than buying everything at the supermarket – you can ask for small portions and it is often more sociable.
- When choosing fruit, choose a mix of ripe and unripe pieces.
- Frozen vegetables stay really fresh and it's easy to take what you need without wasting the rest.

Essential basic foods

The recipes in this book use fresh foods that you are able to buy in small quantities, but they also use longer-life foods that you can keep in your cupboard. Here are some suggestions for your cupboard, fridge and freezer. Only buy those that you like, of course. If you have a window-box or planter, it also makes sense it grow a few herbs as shop-bought ones can be expensive and easily wasted.

Cupboard

Baked beans – for speedy but filling snacks

Baking powder – for cakes and treats

Black peppercorns – for seasoning

Canned sweetcorn – add to salads or eat hot

Canned tomatoes – perfect for sauces and stews

Capers – to add flavour to pizzas and other dishes

Chickpeas or other tinned beans – add to soups and stews

Cornflour – for thickening soups and stews

Couscous – a quick and nutritious meal, just add roast vegetables and olive oil

Curry powder or paste – for added spice

Dried fruit; apricots, cherries, figs, raisins, sultanas – add to breakfast cereals, cakes or biscuits

Dried herbs; bay leaves, coriander, mixed, oregano, rosemary, sage, thyme – to add flavour

Dried tomatoes and/or mushrooms – great for adding flavour

Flour; plain, self-raising, wholemeal – for thickening or baking

Lemons and limes – to squeeze over salads or add to water for a refreshing drink

Noodles – for stir-fries or to add to soups

Oats – good for thickening and to add crunch to toppings

Oil; olive, sunflower or vegetable – for cooking and dressings

Lentils – make a wholesome soup

Nuts/seeds; pine, pumpkin, sesame – add crunch to salads or toppings for stir-fries

Pasta – perfect for a quick and easy meal

Preserves/syrups; honey, jam, lemon curd, maple syrup, treacle – drizzle over fruit for a treat, or add to sweet or savoury dishes

Rice; basmati, long grain, risotto – easy and filling

Root ginger – great for Asian dishes

Salt – for seasoning

Sherry – to add flavour

Spices; cinnamon, cumin, ginger, mixed, nutmeg, paprika – to add flavour

Stock; cubes or liquid, vegetable and/or meat – essential for soups, sauces and stews

Sugar; caster, demerara, icing, soft brown – to sweeten and add to toppings

Tomato purée – great for flavour

Tuna or other canned fish – great for sandwiches, salads and baked potatoes

Vinegar; wine or cider and balsamic – for flavour

Fridge

Butter – for baking and sautéing

Cheese – to nibble on and for melted toppings

Chutney and/or pickle – to jazz up a plain sandwich

Eggs – for a quick snack or baking

Mustard; Dijon, English, wholegrain – great to liven up sandwiches or mash

Olives – a healthy snack or for pizza and pasta

Sauces; mayonnaise, pesto, redcurrant jelly, soy, sweet chilli, tomato ketchup, Worcester – to add flavour

Freezer

Breadcrumbs – whiz old bread in a food processor and use as toppings

Chopped herbs – for flavour

Frozen peas – great for soups and sides

Grated Parmesan – perfect for sprinkling

Tortillas or pitta bread – separate with greaseproof paper and use for sandwiches or pizza

Herb planter

Basil, chives, coriander, dill, mint, parsley, rosemary, sage, tarragon, thyme – essential for salads and flavour

Cook's information

Dry weight conversions

Recommended grams (g)	Imperial ounces (oz)
15	½
25	1
50	2
75	3
110	4 (¼lb)
150	5
175	6
200	7
225	8 (½lb)
250	9
275	10
300	11
350	12 (¾lb)
375	13
400	14
425	15
450	16 (1lb)
500	1lb 2oz
680	1½lb
750	1lb 10oz
900	2lb

These quantities are not exact, but they have been calculated to give proportionately correct measurements.

Liquid conversions

Metric (ml)	Imperial (fl oz)	US cups
15	½	1 tbsp (level)
30	1	⅛
60	2	¼
90	3	⅜
125	4	½
150	5 (¼ pint)	⅔
175	6	¾
225	8	1
300	10 (½ pint)	1¼
350	12	1½
450	16	2
500	18	2¼
600	20 (1 pint)	2½
900	1½ pints	3¾
1 litre	1¾ pints	1 quart (4 cups)
1.25 litres	2 pints	1¼ quarts
1.5 litres	2½ pints	3 US pints
2 litres	3½ pints	2 quarts

568ml = 1 UK pint   (20fl oz)   16fl oz = 1 US pint

These quantities are not exact, but they have been calculated to give proportionately correct measurements.

Suitable for vegetarians

If you are cooking for a vegetarian, please ensure that any cheese, yogurt or pesto sauce you use is suitable for vegetarians. It should give this information on the jar or packet

Guideline daily amounts: adults

	Women	Men
Energy (calories)	2,000	2,500
Fat (g)	70	95
Saturated fat (g)	20	30
Carbohydrate (g)	230	300
Total sugars (g)	90	120
Protein (g)	45	55
Dietary fibre (g)	24	24
Salt (g)	6	6

Oven temperatures

°C	°F	Gas mark	Description
110	225	¼	cool
120/130	250	½	cool
140	275	1	very low
150	300	2	very low
160/170	325	3	low to moderate
180	350	4	moderate
190	375	5	moderately hot
200	400	6	hot
220	425	7	hot
230	450	8	hot
240	475	9	very hot

Guide to recommended equivalent settings, not exact conversions. Always refer to your cooker instruction book.

Grilling times: fish

Type of fish	Grilling time
Cod (steak)	5–6 min each side
Dover sole (whole)	4–6 min each side
Dover sole (fillet)	2–3 min each side
Halibut (steak)	5–6 min each side
Herring (whole)	4–5 min each side
Mackerel (whole)	6–7 min each side
Monkfish (steak)	5–6 min each side
Plaice (whole)	4–6 min each side
Plaice (fillet)	2–3 min each side
Salmon (steak)	5–6 min each side
Tuna (steak)	1–2 min each side

Times given for fish weighing approximately 175–225g (6–8oz).

Roasting times: meat

Set oven temperature to 180°C/350°F/Gas 4.

	Cooking time per 450g/1lb	Extra cooking time
Beef		
Rare	20 min	20 min
Medium	25 min	25 min
Well done	30 min	30 min
Lamb		
Medium	25 min	25 min
Well done	30 min	30 min
Pork		
Medium	30 min	30 min
Well done	35 min	35 min

Let the cooked meat rest for 5–15 minutes before carving to allow the juices to be reabsorbed and to make carving easier.

Steaming times: vegetables

Vegetable	Steaming time
Asparagus	5–7 min
Beansprouts	3–4 min
Beetroot (sliced)	5–7 min
Broccoli (florets)	5–7 min
Brussel sprouts	5–7 min
Cabbage (chopped)	4–6 min
Cauliflower (florets)	5–7 min
Carrots (thickly sliced)	5–7 min
Courgettes (sliced)	3–5 min
Green beans	5–7 min
Leeks	5–8 min
Mangetout peas	3–5 min
Peas	3–5 min
Potatoes (cubed)	5–7 min

Times given are for steaming from when water has started to boil.

Roasting times: poultry

	Oven temperature	Cooking time per 450g/1lb	Extra cooking time	Resting time
Chicken	200°C/400°F/Gas 6	20 min	30 min	15 min
Turkey (stuffed weight)				
small (under 6kg/13lb)	200°C/400°F/Gas 6	12 min	20 min	30 min
large	180°C/350°F/Gas 4	16 min	—	30 min
Duck	200°C/400°F/Gas 6 for 45 min then 180°C/350°F/Gas 4	35 min	—	15 min

Soups and light meals

Soup has a long history, with the earliest recipes dating back 8,000 years. In the Middle Ages a thick soup known as pottage was the dietary mainstay for most of the population. And in Jane Austen's novels guests were welcomed from their cold journey by a tureen of hot soup.

Nothing lasts that long without being pretty good, and soup is one of the great comfort foods: warming, nutritious, easy to eat and digest – and infinitely variable.

The soups in this chapter really are scrumptious and much better than anything you would find in a can. In addition to soups, this chapter also offers a range of snacks so tasty – and simple to prepare – that you will vow to give those beans on toast a miss today and really treat your tastebuds at lunchtime.

Preparation time	**10 minutes**
Cooking time	**20 minutes**
Calories per portion	**558 Kcal**
Fat per portion	**23g**
of which saturated	**5g**
Serves	**1**

Suitable for vegetarians + freezing

Italian-style bean soup

Olive oil 1 tbsp
Onion 1 small, peeled and chopped
Garlic 1 clove, peeled and crushed
Chopped tomatoes 227g can
Dried oregano ½ tsp
Kidney beans 220g can, drained and rinsed
Vegetable stock 300ml (½ pint)

Green beans 50g (2oz)
topped, tailed and halved
Salt and freshly ground black pepper
Plain or olive flavoured ciabatta roll
1, cut into 4 thick slices
Pesto sauce 2 tbsp

1   Heat the oil in a saucepan and gently fry the onion and garlic for 4–5 minutes until softened but not browned. Stir in the tomatoes, oregano and kidney beans. Bring to the boil, cover and simmer very gently for 10 minutes.

2   Meanwhile, pour the stock into another small saucepan and bring to the boil. Add the green beans, cover and cook for 5 minutes until just tender. Add the cooking stock along with the cooked beans to the tomato mixture. Stir well, season and keep warm over a low heat while preparing the toasts.

3   Preheat the grill to hot. Line the grill tray with foil and arrange the ciabatta on the foil. Cook under the grill for 2–3 minutes until lightly toasted. Spread with pesto sauce and grill for a few seconds longer until piping hot.

4   Ladle the soup into a warm bowl and eat immediately with the toasted pesto ciabatta.

13

Preparation time	**1 minute**
Cooking time	**5 minutes**
Calories per portion	**243 Kcal**
Fat per portion	**13g**
of which saturated	**1.8g**
Serves	**1**
Suitable for vegetarians	

Bruschetta with roasted vine tomatoes

Ciabatta roll halved, then sliced lengthways and use one piece
Cherry or plum tomatoes on the vine 5–8, depending on their size
Olive oil 1 tbsp
Garlic 1 clove, unpeeled
Balsamic or sherry vinegar good dash
Freshly ground black pepper
Basil leaves a few, optional

1 Preheat the oven to 200°C/400°F/Gas 6. Put the bread and the tomatoes in a small roasting tin and drizzle with the olive oil.

2 Roast for 10 minutes, turning the bread and checking the tomatoes about halfway through cooking.

3 Halve the clove of garlic and rub it over the cooked bread (discard the garlic afterwards). Put the toasted bread on a large plate and place the tomatoes on top. Spoon any pan juices over and add a dash of vinegar, grind some black pepper on top and garnish with a few basil leaves, if using.

Cook's tip
Use the leftover ciabatta for a scrumptious sandwich, or whizz in a food processor and store the breadcrumbs in the freezer.

Shopper's tip
Get the best-quality tomatoes you can afford – pome dei moro are really sweet and juicy for roasting.

Preparation time	**10 minutes**
Cooking time	**15 minutes**
Calories per portion	**585 Kcal**
Fat per portion	**31g**
of which saturated	**16g**
Serves	**1**

Pasta with smoked salmon cream sauce

Linguine pasta 75g (3oz)
Olive oil 1 tsp
Spring onion 1, trimmed, washed and finely sliced
Smoked salmon or smoked trout 50g (2oz), chopped
Whipping cream 4–5 tbsp
Freshly ground black pepper
Lime wedge

1   Cook the pasta in a pan of lightly salted boiling water according to the packet instructions and drain. Meanwhile, heat the oil and fry the spring onion until softened.

2   Stir in the chopped salmon and whipping cream and heat until beginning to bubble. Bring the mixture to the boil and simmer for a minute or two, stirring frequently.

3   Stir the cooked pasta into the sauce, season with pepper and serve with the lime wedge on a fork for squeezing before eating.

Cook's tip
To use up leftover ingredients, beat 50g (2oz) smoked salmon into 2 eggs and add 3 tbsp double cream. Cook gently in melted butter, stirring, until set.

Shopper's tip
A 110g (4oz) pack of smoked salmon makes this recipe and the luxury scrambled egg above.

Preparation time	**5 minutes**
Calories per portion	**300 Kcal**
Fat per portion	**24g**
of which saturated	**3.8g**
Serves	**1**

Prawns with 'British' mayo

Mayonnaise 2 tbsp
Horseradish relish or sauce ½ tsp
Wholegrain mustard ½ tsp
Worcestershire sauce or Tabasco sauce a good dash

North Atlantic cooked prawns in their shells 200g (7oz)
Little gem lettuce 1, cut lengthways into quarters
Lemon or lime wedge, optional

1   In a small bowl, mix the mayonnaise with the horseradish, mustard and Worcestershire or Tabasco sauce.

2   Put the prawns on a plate and then put the mayonnaise bowl on the plate together with the lettuce and a wedge of lemon or lime, if using. Put a bowl for the empty shells and a napkin on the plate as well.

3   To eat, peel your prawns and dip them in the sauce. Dip the lettuce wedges as well.

Cook's tip
Make a spicy dip by adding a very small clove of garlic, peeled and crushed, and fresh chilli or dried chilli flakes, to taste.

Shopper's tip
Buy a small jar of mayonnaise and, once opened, keep it in the fridge. It will last for a couple of months.

Preparation time	**5 minutes**
Calories per portion	**219 Kcal**
Fat per portion	**16g**
of which saturated	**3.4g**
Serves	**1**

Prosciutto ham and peach with wild rocket

Prosciutto crudo ham 3 slices
Peach 1, halved, stoned and sliced
Rocket 15g (½oz)
Olive oil 1 tbsp
Lime ½ small, juice only
Freshly ground black pepper

1 Cut each slice of ham in half lengthways and arrange carefully in a circle on a plate with the sliced peaches, leaving the centre for the wild rocket. Arrange the rocket attractively.

2 Drizzle with the olive oil and freshly squeezed lime juice and add a scattering of black pepper.

Cook's tip
Use the remaining slices of prosciutto to wrap around a slice of honeydew melon for a quick and light starter.

Shopper's tip
Prosciutto is Italian air-dried ham. It is usually sold in packs of five slices and will keep for a week in the fridge once opened.

Preparation time	**5 minutes**
Cooking time	**15 minutes**
Calories per portion	**645 Kcal**
Fat per portion	**42g**
of which saturated	**8.3g**
Serves	**1**

Brunchtime French toasts

Egg 1, beaten
Salt and freshly ground black pepper
Wholemeal bread 1 slice
Vegetable oil 2 tbsp
Lean trimmed back bacon 2 rashers, de-rinded
Field mushroom 1, wiped, peeled and sliced
Tomato 1, thickly sliced
Snipped chives to garnish

1   Beat the egg with 2 tablespoons of water and some seasoning and then pour onto a plate. Dip the bread on both sides in the egg, allowing it to soak up all the mixture.

2   Melt the butter with the oil in a frying pan until bubbling, then cook the bread for 2–3 minutes on each side until lightly golden and set. Drain well, reserving the pan juices, and keep warm.

3   Add the bacon to the pan and cook for 3–4 minutes on each side until cooked through and lightly golden. Drain well, reserving the pan juices, and keep warm.

4   Add the sliced mushroom and tomato to the pan and cook, turning occasionally, for about 5 minutes until cooked through and tender.

5   To serve, place the eggy bread on to a warm serving plate and top with the bacon, tomato, mushrooms and snipped chives. Eat immediately.

Cook's tip
If preferred, replace the bacon with pork sausages or a vegetarian variety for a tasty veggie version.

Shopper's tip
Slice loaves of bread, pack loosely in a freezer bag and freeze. Take out individual slices at your convenience.

Preparation time	**30 minutes**
Cooking time	**30 minutes**
Chilling time	**2–3 hours**
Calories per portion	**273 Kcal**
Fat per portion	**15g**
of which saturated	**3.2g**
Serves	**2**

Suitable for vegetarians + freezing

Chilled asparagus soup with oven-baked croutons

For the croutons
White or wholemeal bread 1 thick slice, crusts removed and cut into small cubes

For the soup
Sunflower oil 1 tbsp
Onion 1, peeled and separated into rings
Courgettes 2, trimmed and thinly sliced
Asparagus spears 8, woody ends snapped or cut off and stems cut into 1cm (½in) pieces, keeping the spears whole

Beefsteak tomato 1 large, skinned, deseeded and diced
Vegetable stock 450ml (¾ pint)
Salt and freshly ground black pepper

To serve
Chopped parsley 1 tbsp
Finely shredded basil 1 tbsp
Snipped chives 1 tbsp
Olive oil 1 tbsp

1 Preheat the oven to190°C/375°F/Gas 5. Spread the bread cubes evenly on a baking tray and then bake in oven for 10–15 minutes, or until just lightly browned. Remove the croutons from the oven and allow to cool.

2 Heat the sunflower oil in a large saucepan, add the onion rings and cook over a medium heat until softened, out not browned. Add the courgettes and continue cooking for 2–3 minutes.

3 Add the asparagus stems, diced tomato and stock to the saucepan. Bring the soup up to the boil, then reduce the heat, cover and cook gently for 10 minutes. Then add the asparagus spears and continue cooking for another 5 minutes, or until the vegetables are only just cooked and retain a slightly crisp texture.

4 Season the soup to taste, allow to cool and then chill well for 2–3 hours. Before serving, gently stir in the herbs and olive oil. Serve the soup in individual bowls, sprinkled with the croutons.

Cook's tip
Turn leftover soup into a starter. Strain the soup and reduce liquid by two-thirds, cool and pour over the veg. Serve chilled with toast.

Shopper's tip
Young thin asparagus stems are best or cut larger stems in half lengthways. Day-old bread is best served as croutons.

Preparation time	10 minutes
Cooking time	30 minutes
Calories per portion	186 Kcal
Fat per portion	10g
of which saturated	2.1g
Serves	2

Suitable for vegetarians + freezing

Spaghetti soup

1. Heat the olive oil in a large saucepan, add the onion and carrot and cook over a medium heat for about 5 minutes or until the vegetables have started to soften. Add the mushrooms to the pan and cook for a further 2–3 minutes.

2. Add the canned tomatoes, stock cube and water to the pan and bring the mixture to the boil. Reduce the heat, cover the pan and simmer the soup for 12–15 minutes or until the vegetables are tender. Break the spaghetti or noodles into pieces and add to the pan, then boil the soup, uncovered, for 2–3 minutes, or until the pasta is cooked.

3. Stir half of the pesto into the soup and season to taste with salt and pepper. Pour into a serving bowl and sprinkle with the Parmesan cheese and remaining pesto just before serving.

Olive oil 1 tbsp
Onion 1 small, peeled and sliced
Carrot 1, peeled and diced
Button mushrooms 4–6, wiped and chopped
Chopped tomatoes 227g can
Vegetable stock cube 1

Boiling water 600ml (1 pint)
Angel hair spaghetti or rice noodles 25g (1oz)
Pesto sauce 1 tbsp
Salt and freshly ground black pepper
Grated Parmesan-like cheese ½–1 tbsp

Cook's tip
If the soup thickens too much, add a little extra boiling water. The soup may thicken after freezing; again, add more water.

Shopper's tip
You can use ordinary spaghetti, but it will need to be added at the beginning of step 2. You may need to add more water.

Cook's tip

The soup can be made in advance and stored in a covered container in the refrigerator. Reheat thoroughly.

Shopper's tip

For the very best flavour, choose red, ripe tomatoes.

Preparation time	**30 minutes**
Cooking time	**45 minutes**
Calories per portion	**237 Kcal**
Fat per portion	**15g**
of which saturated	**1.6g**
Serves	**2**

Suitable for vegetarians + freezing

Red pepper and tomato soup

Beefsteak tomatoes 2 large
Olive oil 2 tbsp
Red pepper 1 large, deseeded and cut into thin strips
Onion 1 large, peeled and thinly sliced
Sun-dried tomato paste 1 tbsp

Orange 1 large, finely grated zest and juice
Vegetable stock 600ml (1 pint)
Salt and freshly ground black pepper
Single or double cream 1 tbsp, optional
Sun-dried tomato or olive ciabatta to serve, optional

1. Using a small, sharp pointed knife and cutting at a slight angle, cut out a cone shape from the stalk end of each tomato to remove the white, woody centre.

2. Put the tomatoes into a heatproof bowl, cover them with boiling water and leave to stand for 2 minutes. Using a slotted spoon, remove the tomatoes from the water and leave to cool. When cool enough to handle, remove the skins. Cut each tomato in half and remove the seeds – using a small teaspoon or round-bladed knife – then roughly chop the flesh.

3. Heat the olive oil in a large saucepan, add the red pepper and onion and cook gently for 5 minutes, or until slightly softened, but not browned. Add the chopped tomatoes, sun-dried tomato paste, orange zest and juice, and stock to the saucepan.

4. Bring the soup up to the boil, reduce the heat, cover the pan and cook gently for about 45 minutes, or until the peppers and onions are softened. Remove the pan from the heat and allow the soup to cool. Purée the soup, in batches, in a food processor or blender.

5. If you like, place a large sieve over a clean saucepan and use the back of a wooden spoon to pass the soup through the sieve to remove the coarser pieces of skin from the peppers.

6. Reheat the soup, season to taste and garnish with a little cream, if using, and coarsely ground black pepper. Serve immediately, accompanied with warm, sun-dried tomato or olive ciabatta bread.

Preparation time	**40 minutes**
Cooking time	**30–40 minutes**
Calories per portion	**739 Kcal**
Fat per portion	**42g**
of which saturated	**20.1g**
Serves	**2**
Suitable for vegetarians	

Eggs au gratin

Eggs 4 large
Butter 25g (1oz)
Spring onions 4 large, trimmed,
washed and thinly sliced
Plain flour 25g (1oz)
Milk 300ml (½ pint)
**Double Gloucester or Cheddar
cheese** 75–110g (3–4oz), grated
Double cream 2 tbsp, optional
**Salt and freshly ground black
pepper**
Tomatoes 2–3, sliced
White breadcrumbs 3 rounded tbsp
Rolled oats 3 rounded tbsp

1 Preheat the oven to 180°C/350°F/Gas 5. Put the eggs into a small saucepan, cover with cold water, bring to the boil and boil gently for 10 minutes. Remove the eggs from the pan and cool in cold water until cold. Shell the eggs, then cut them in half lengthways and arrange, cut sides down, in a lightly buttered, shallow 1 litre (1¾ pint) gratin dish or pie dish.

2 To make the sauce, melt the butter in a saucepan, add the spring onions and cook gently for 2–3 minutes until softened, but not browned. Stir the flour into the butter and onions, add the milk and bring slowly up to the boil, stirring continuously until the sauce thickens. Add two-thirds of the cheese and the cream, if using, and stir well until the cheese melts. Season to taste.

3 Pour the sauce evenly over the eggs. Arrange the sliced tomatoes over the top. Mix together the breadcrumbs, oats and remaining cheese and sprinkle evenly over the sauce. Bake in the oven for 30–40 minutes, until golden brown and bubbling hot.

Cook's tip
This dish may be prepared well in advance of baking. Cool, then cover and refrigerate. Allow extra time when reheating.

Shopper's tip
If you enjoy a richly flavoured sauce, buy extra mature cheese.

Preparation time	**10 minutes**
Cooking time	**6 minutes**
Calories per portion	**485 Kcal**
Fat per portion	**28g**
of which saturated	**4.2g**
Serves	**2**

Suitable for vegetarians

Sweetcorn fritters with avocado and tomato salsa

For the fritters
Self-raising flour 4 tbsp
Egg 1
Milk 2–3 tbsp
Sweetcorn 198g can, drained
Salt and freshly ground black pepper
Sunflower oil 1 tbsp

For the salsa
Lime 1, grated zest and juice
Olive oil 1 tbsp
Avocado 1, stoned, peeled and finely chopped
Tomatoes 2, deseeded and finely chopped
Finely chopped coriander 1 tbsp
Chilli sauce a dash

1. To make the fritters, tip the flour into a bowl and beat in the egg and enough milk to give a thick, smooth batter. Stir in the sweetcorn and seasoning.

2. Heat the sunflower oil in a large frying pan. Spoon the sweetcorn batter into the pan into four rounds. Cook the fritters for 2–3 minutes, then turn them over and cook for a further 2–3 minutes until they are a golden colour and cooked through. Remove them from the pan.

3. To make the salsa, put the lime zest and juice and olive oil in a bowl and mix them together, then stir in the avocado, tomatoes and coriander. Add the chilli sauce and seasoning to taste. Serve two fritters on each plate with the salsa spooned on top.

Cook's tip
Don't make the batter too runny or the fritters will spread out too much in the pan, and may all merge into one.

Shopper's tip
If you don't have any fresh coriander, then look out for coriander purée in a tube, which will last for several weeks.

Preparation time	**5 minutes**
Cooking time	**25 minutes**
Calories per portion	**319 Kcal**
Fat per portion	**25g**
of which saturated	**4.5g**
Serves	**2**

Tuna stuffed mushrooms

Flat mushrooms 2 large, wiped and stalks removed and finely chopped
Bread roll 1 small
Tuna 80g can, drained
Shallot 1, peeled and finely chopped

Salad dressing 4 tbsp
Chopped parsley 1 tbsp
Grated Parmesan cheese 1 tbsp
Salt and freshly ground black pepper

1. Preheat the oven to 200°C/400°F/Gas 6. Place the mushrooms on a baking sheet, curved sides down.

2. To make the filling, tear the bread roll into small pieces and place in a bowl. Add the mushroom stalks, tuna, shallot, salad dressing, parsley, Parmesan cheese and seasoning and mix together. Spoon the filling onto the mushrooms and press it down well.

3. Bake the mushrooms in the centre of the oven for 20–25 minutes, until the topping is golden and the mushrooms feel tender when pierced with a fine knife. Serve immediately either on their own or with some green salad.

Cook's tip
Most flavours of salad dressing will work well in this recipe, particularly if it is made with balsamic vinegar.

Shopper's tip
If you do not have fresh parsley, buy a small packet, chop and freeze any that you have not used in the recipe.

27

Perfect portions

There are few things a cook dislikes more than throwing out perfectly good food, and this fare is designed to provide just the right amount to satisfy your appetite, with absolutely no fussing about leftovers.

For those midweek meals, where you want quick food without fuss and, of course, without waste, this chapter is perfect. There are recipes to suit every palate: from prawn kebabs to rack of lamb with unusual combinations such as pasta with pine nuts, blue cheese and raisins.

There's a mix of vegetarian dishes, fish, meat and poultry, so there is plenty of variety to tempt you.

Preparation time	5 minutes
Cooking time	10 minutes
Calories per portion	376 Kcal
Fat per portion	21g
of which saturated	6.8g
Serves	1
Suitable for vegetarians	

Sweet potato rosti with poached egg

For the rosti
Sweet potato 1, peeled and grated
Egg 1
Salt and freshly ground black pepper
Sunflower oil 1 tsp
Butter small knob

For the egg
Egg 1
Vinegar a dash

To serve
Chopped chives a few

For the rosti, mix the potato, egg and seasoning in a bowl. Press the mixture into a patty shape.

Heat a small frying pan, and add the sunflower oil and butter. Slide the sweet potato rosti into the pan, re-shaping it if necessary. Cook for 3–5 minutes, and slide a palette knife or fish slice under it to make sure it hasn't stuck to the base of the pan. Then place a small plate over it and turn the pan over so the rosti drops out onto the plate. Slide the rosti off the plate back into the pan and cook it for a further 3–5 minutes, until cooked through and golden.

Meanwhile, prepare the egg. Break the egg into a cup or small bowl. Heat some water in a small saucepan and add a dash of vinegar. When the water comes to the boil, use a spoon to stir the water to swirl it around, and then when the water is still spinning, tip the egg into the centre of it. Cook the egg for 3–4 minutes or until the white has set, but the yolk is runny. Remove the egg from the pan with a slotted spoon.

Slide the rosti onto a serving plate and place the egg on top. Scatter with a few chopped chives and season the top with pepper.

Cook's tip
Instead of poaching the egg directly in simmering water, you can use an egg poaching tin with removable cups.

Shopper's tip
Buy eggs that are as fresh as possible because their whites are firmer and keep a better shape when poaching.

Preparation time	**10 minutes**
Cooking time	**20 minutes**
Calories per portion	**542 Kcal**
Fat per portion	**29g**
of which saturated	**16.3g**
Serves	**1**
Suitable for vegetarians	

Mushroom risotto

Melt the butter in a medium-sized saucepan, add the onion and cook for about 5 minutes over a medium heat until it starts to soften. Add the mushrooms and cook for a further 3–4 minutes, until softened.

Tip the rice into the pan and cook for about 1 minute, stirring continuously. Add the soup and boiling water and bring the mixture to the boil. Reduce the heat and simmer the risotto for about 15 minutes, stirring it frequently until it's thickened and the rice is tender. If it appears too dry, then add a little extra boiling water.

Stir the parsley and seasoning into the rice just before serving. Spoon the risotto onto a serving plate and sprinkle with the Parmesan cheese.

Butter 15g (½oz)
Onion 1 small, peeled and sliced
Button mushrooms 2–3, wiped and sliced
Risotto rice 50g (2oz)
Condensed mushroom soup 295g can

Boiling water 150ml (¼ pint)
Chopped parsley 1 tbsp
Salt and freshly ground black pepper
Grated or shaved Parmesan-like cheese to serve

Cook's tip
Stirring the risotto regularly during cooking helps to develop the characteristic stickiness of the rice.

Shopper's tip
Any tin of condensed soup will work – try chicken or celery. If you don't have risotto rice, then use pudding rice instead.

Preparation time	5 minutes
Cooking time	5 minutes
Calories per portion	481 Kcal
Fat per portion	39g
of which saturated	16.6g
Serves	1
Suitable for vegetarians	

Brie and chive omelette

Eggs 3
Salt and freshly ground black pepper
Chives about 12 stems
Butter a knob
Brie (or Camembert) 50g (2oz), rind left on
Watercress or rocket leaves to serve

Lightly beat the eggs in a bowl until just mixed. Add seasoning and use scissors to snip the chives straight in – you are aiming for about 2 tablespoons of the chopped chives.

Heat a frying pan, add the butter and when it sizzles snake the pan to swirl the butter around. Turn down the heat a little and pour the eggs into the pan. Move the pan around so the eggs are spread out evenly and cook for 1–2 minutes until the omelette is beginning to set.

Snip the cheese with scissors in rough cubes over the omelette. Leave on a low heat for 30 seconds, then, using a spatula, fold one-third of the omelette to the middle, then the other third over and slide it onto a plate. Serve with some watercress or rocket leaves.

Cook's tip
Using this recipe to serve two? Double the quantities but then make two separate omelettes rather than one large one.

Shopper's tip
Buy unwashed watercress or rocket, if available, and soak the leaves in very cold water for 20 minutes until they perk up.

Preparation time	5 minutes
Cooking time	10 minutes
Calories per portion	878 Kcal
Fat per portion	38g
of which saturated	20.1g
Serves	1

Suitable for vegetarians

Pasta with crunchy crumbs and feta

Tagliatelle or spaghetti 75g (3oz)
Butter 25g (1oz)
White breadcrumbs (day old or from the freezer), 6 tbsp
Lemon ½
Feta cheese 50g (2oz), cubed or roughly crumbled
Chopped parsley a good handful
Salt and freshly ground black pepper
Olive oil for drizzling

Pour boiling water into a large pan, add some salt and the pasta and cook according to the pack instructions.

Meanwhile, heat the butter in a small saucepan and when sizzling add the breadcrumbs and cook for about 5 minutes, stirring occasionally until crisp and golden. Use a zester (or grater) to grate the lemon zest into the crumbs. Cut the lemon half into two wedges and set aside.

Drain the pasta, put it back in the pan, toss in the crumb mixture, add the feta cheese chunks, parsley and seasoning.

Serve in a large warm bowl drizzled with olive oil and with the lemon wedges on the side. Squeeze lemon juice over as you eat the pasta to bring out the flavour.

Cook's tip
Pasta packs often recommend 75–110g (3–4oz) pasta per serving; for a smaller appetite, cut it down to 50g (2oz).

Shopper's tip
Once opened and drained, feta packs don't keep long. Look out for tubs of feta cubes instead; the cheese keeps longer.

Preparation time	**30 minutes**
Cooking time	**6–8 minutes**
Calories per portion	**174 Kcal**
Fat per portion	**12g**
of which saturated	**1.6g**
Serves	**1**

Prawn and scallop kebabs

Large tiger prawns 2–3
Prepared scallops 2–3, washed and dried
Sunflower oil 1–2 tbsp
Chopped dill 1 tbsp (or 1 tsp freeze-dried)

Freshly ground black pepper
Romaine lettuce 1–2 of the larger leaves plus extra to serve
New potatoes to serve, optional

Remove the heads and peel the prawns – leaving the tail shell on. Slit them and remove the black vein from the back. Place the shelled prawns in a mixing bowl, add the scallops, oil and dill, then season well with pepper and mix gently until evenly coated.

Preheat the grill to hot. Cut the lettuce leaf (or leaves) lenghways into two or three strips. Thread one of the prawns onto a skewer, approximately 23–25cm (9–10in) long. Wrap a piece of lettuce around a scallop and thread it onto the skewer.

Thread the remaining prawns and scallops onto the skewer in the same way. Place the kebab on a rack in the grill pan and brush with the remaining oil mixture. Cook for 2–3 minutes, turning the kebab over after 2 minutes (or when the prawns turn pink) and cook the other side for 1 minute, or until pink. Serve with new potatoes and a few lettuce leaves.

Cook's tip
If preferred, cubes of fresh haddock, cod or tuna may be used instead of scallops – or use extra prawns.

Shopper's tip
Buy fresh fish and shellfish on the day you wish to use them. Alternatively, buy and freeze, then thaw on the day.

Preparation time	30 minutes
Cooking time	30 minutes
Calories per portion	614 Kcal
Fat per portion	18g
of which saturated	5.2g
Serves	1

Cod with a light curry sauce

Long grain rice 50g (2oz)
Salt and freshly ground black pepper
Sunflower oil 2 tsp
Onion 1 small, peeled and finely chopped
Curry paste, mild-medium hot 1–1½ tsp
Beefsteak tomato 1 large, skinned, deseeded and chopped
Prime cod or haddock fillet 225–350g (8–12oz)
Apricot jam 1 rounded tbsp
Single or double cream 2 tbsp
Coriander sprigs to garnish, optional
Naan bread to serve, optional

Preheat the oven to 220°C/425°F/Gas 7. Put the rice in a small saucepan, add 150ml (¼ pint) cold water and a pinch of salt. Bring to the boil, cover the pan with a lid, reduce the heat to low and cook for 20–25 minutes, or until all the water is absorbed and the rice is cooked.

Meanwhile, heat the oil in a medium-sized saucepan, add the onion and cook gently until softened, but not browned. Add the curry paste and chopped tomato, cover the pan and cook gently until the tomato is soft and pulpy, stirring frequently for 10–15 minutes.

While the rice and sauce are cooking, place the cod or haddock fillet on a sheet of lightly oiled foil and season well with salt and pepper. Enclose the fish in the foil, place on a baking tray and cook in the oven for 15–20 minutes – until it is only just cooked (when it turns opaque, but is still slightly translucent – take care not to overcook as the fillet will break up).

While the fish is cooking, add the jam and cream to the curry sauce, season to taste and keep hot, but do not allow it to boil.

When the fish and the rice are both cooked, spoon the rice onto a warmed serving plate. Arrange the fish on top of the rice (don't worry if it breaks up). Pour the sauce over the top, or around the rice, and garnish with coriander sprigs, if using. Serve with warmed naan bread.

Cook's tip
If you don't have foil to hand for baking the fish, you can use lightly oiled baking parchment instead.

Shopper's tip
Buy a small tub of cream and use any leftovers stirred through pasta and roast vegetables.

Preparation time	**10 minutes**
Cooking time	**10–12 minutes**
Calories per portion	**565 Kcal**
Fat per portion	**32g**
of which saturated	**5.1g**
Serves	**1**

Perfect portions

Haddock with poached egg

Ciabatta loaf quarter piece, or a thick slice of any day-old bread, torn into pieces
Olive oil 2 tbsp
Fine green beans 50g (2oz), trimmed and halved
Smoked haddock 1 piece weighing about 150g (5oz)
White wine or cider vinegar 2 tsp
Egg 1
Wholegrain mustard 1 tsp
Salt and freshly ground black pepper

Preheat the grill to hot. Scatter the pieces of bread on a baking sheet and sprinkle with 1 tablespoon of the oil. Use your hand to coat the bread roughly in oil. Toast under the grill for 4–5 minutes until crispy and browned. Do watch the bread pieces don't burn by turning them a couple of times.

Meanwhile, half fill a medium-sized saucepan with boiling water. Bring the water back to the boil and add the beans. Cook them for 3 minutes in the boiling water, then take them out with a draining spoon and put into a small bowl. Add the other tablespoon of oil to the warm beans and coat them with it.

Add the fish to the pan, cover and poach gently at a simmer over a low heat for 3–5 minutes, depending on its thickness. Take the fish out with a fish slice and put it onto a piece of kitchen paper on a warm plate.

Add a splash of the vinegar to the pan of water, bring back to the boil and crack the egg into the water. Poach it for 3 minutes, or to your liking.

Meanwhile, skin and break the fish into large flakes and put on the plate (discard the kitchen paper first!) with the ciabatta croutons and beans, removed from the oil using a slotted spoon. Place the poached egg on top. Whisk the rest of the vinegar and the mustard into the reserved oil, then drizzle the whole dish with this dressing. Season with a little salt and lots of pepper.

Cook's tip
Ingredients are easily doubled if you want to make this recipe for two or it can be 'bulked out' by adding salad or spinach leaves.

Shopper's tip
Buy fish and pop it in the freezer in manageable pieces as it can be thawed and cooked quickly for solo meals.

Preparation time	5 minutes
Cooking time	20 minutes
Calories per portion	609 Kcal
Fat per portion	45g
of which saturated	18g
Serves	1

Mackerel with lime and caper sauce and crushed potatoes

New potatoes 4, scrubbed
Butter 25g (1oz)
Mackerel 1, filleted
Salt and freshly ground black pepper
Lime 1, grated zest and juice

Capers 1 tbsp, drained and roughly chopped
Spring onions 2–3, trimmed, washed and sliced

Bring a medium-sized saucepan of water to the boil and add the new potatoes. Bring the water back to the boil, then reduce the heat to low and cook the potatoes for 15–18 minutes, or until they are tender.

Meanwhile, melt the butter in a frying pan over a medium heat. Score the skin of the mackerel into a criss-cross pattern and season the flesh side of the fillets. Add the mackerel to the pan, skin-side down, and cook the fish for 2–3 minutes or until the skin starts to crisp, then turn the fillets over and cook for a further 1–2 minutes, or until the fish is cooked. Remove the fillets from the pan and add the lime zest and juice, capers and spring onions and cook over a low heat for 1–2 minutes. Season to taste.

Drain the potatoes well and then return them to the pan and use a spoon to crush them against the side of the pan until they split open.

Spoon the potatoes onto a serving plate and place the fish fillets on top. Pour over the lime and caper sauce, so that any juices will be absorbed into the potatoes, and serve immediately.

Cook's tip
When you're cooking the potatoes, you could cook a few extra and use them cold as the basis of a potato salad.

Shopper's tip
To save time preparing the recipe at home, ask the fishmonger to fillet the mackerel for you when you buy it.

Preparation time	5 minutes
Cooking time	25 minutes
Calories per portion	620 Kcal
Fat per portion	19g
of which saturated	3.8g
Serves	1

One-pan pasta for one

Sunflower oil 1 tbsp
Skinless chicken breast
1 (approximately 200g/7oz),
chopped
Courgette 1 small, trimmed
and roughly chopped
Red pepper 1 small, deseeded
and sliced
Garlic 1 clove, peeled and

crushed, optional
Chopped tomatoes 227g can
Boiling water 150ml (¼ pint)
Pasta shapes 50g (2oz)
Pesto sauce 1 tbsp
**Salt and freshly ground
black pepper**
Garlic bread to serve, optional

Heat the sunflower oil in a medium-sized saucepan and add the chicken. Cook the chicken for 1–2 minutes until it turns white, turning it occasionally, then add the courgette and red pepper, and the garlic, if using. Cook over a medium heat for 5–7 minutes, stirring regularly, until the vegetables have softened and the chicken is starting to brown.

Add the canned tomatoes and boiling water and bring the mixture to the boil. Add the pasta to the pan and cook over a medium heat for about 15 minutes or until the pasta is tender. Stir the mixture occasionally, particularly as it starts to thicken, so it does not catch and burn on the base of the pan.

Stir in the pesto sauce and season to taste before serving with garlic bread.

Cook's tip
If the sauce starts to thicken too much, add a little boiling water. Different pastas absorb different amounts of liquid.

Shopper's tip
Any pasta shape can be used in this recipe, but it works particularly well with trottole or spirals.

Preparation time	**20 minutes**
Cooking time	**30 minutes**
Calories per portion	**948 Kcal**
Fat per portion	**40g**
of which saturated	**17g**
Serves	**1**

American-style chicken

Put the rice into a small saucepan, add 150ml (¼ pint) cold water and a good pinch of salt. Bring to the boil, then cover the pan, reduce the heat to low and cook for 15–20 minutes or until the rice is cooked, adding the sweetcorn after 10 minutes.

Meanwhile, put the flour onto a plate, add seasoning and the paprika and mix together. Coat the chicken thighs well in the seasoned flour, then shake off the excess.

Put the butter and sunflower oil into a heavy based frying pan and heat until hot, taking care not to let the butter burn. Place the chicken thighs, skin-side down, in the pan and cook gently for 2–3 minutes until golden brown, then turn them over and brown the other sides.

Reduce the heat under the pan, cover with a lid and cook for 10–15 more minutes until the thighs are cooked through. Then remove from pan onto a serving plate, cover and keep warm.

Pour off excess fat from pan, then add the chicken stock and bring to the boil, stirring and scraping browned residue from the bottom of the pan. Stir the cream into the sauce and then strain through a small sieve over the chicken thighs. Mix the chives and parsley into the rice and serve with the chicken thighs.

Long grain rice 50g (2oz)
Salt and freshly ground black pepper
Prepared corncob 1, kernels carefully cut away from the side of the cob with a sharp knife
Plain flour 25g (1oz)
Paprika ½ tsp

Chicken thighs 4 small or 2 large
Butter 15g (½oz)
Sunflower oil 1 tbsp
Chicken stock 225ml (8fl oz)
Double cream 2–3 tbsp
Snipped chives 1–2 tsp
Chopped parsley 1 tbsp

Cook's tip
When cheap, buy corn cobs and blanch in boiling water for 6–8 minutes. When cool, cut away the kernels and freeze.

Shopper's tip
When choosing fresh, ready prepared corn cobs, look for those that have plump and fresh looking kernels.

41

Preparation time	20 minutes
Cooking time	15–20 minutes
Calories per portion	485 Kcal
Fat per portion	13g
of which saturated	7g
Serves	1

Pan-fried chicken breast with dried figs

Skinless chicken breast 1 (approximately 200g/7oz)
Salt and freshly ground black pepper
Butter 25g (1oz)
Lemon ½, juice only

White wine 125ml (4fl oz)
Dried ready-to-eat figs 3–4, halved
Honey 1 tbsp
Dijon mustard ½ tsp
Broccoli to serve, optional

Using a sharp knife, lightly make two long cuts in the rounded side of the chicken breast, then season well with salt and pepper.

Melt the butter in a small frying pan, place the chicken breast, scored-side down, in the butter and cook over a medium heat for 3–4 minutes until lightly browned. Turn over the chicken breast and cook the other side for another 3–4 minutes, until the breast is no longer pink in the centre, taking care not to over-cook. Transfer the chicken breast from the pan onto a serving plate and keep warm in a low oven.

Skim off any excess fat from the pan juices, then add the lemon juice, white wine and figs. Bring to the boil, stirring and scraping any residue from the bottom of the pan. Transfer the figs onto the plate with the chicken.

Add the honey and mustard to the pan juices and then bring to the boil and boil gently, stirring continuously, until the sauce is slightly reduced and thickened. Strain the juices through a small nylon sieve over the chicken and serve immediately with steamed broccoli.

Cook's tip
Keep the remaining lemon half in a ramekin dish cut-side down and use it to bring out the flavour of fish or in a dressing.

Shopper's tip
For the best flavour, buy organic, free-range chicken breast fillets.

Preparation time	**5 minutes**
Cooking time	**25 minutes**
Calories per portion	**842 Kcal**
Fat per portion	**50g**
of which saturated	**18.4g**
Serves	**1**

Pork chop with sage and apple sauce and balsamic chips

Butter 15g (½oz)
Onion 1, peeled and coarsely chopped
Caster sugar 1 tsp
Cooking apple 1 small, peeled, cored and chopped
Dried sage 1 tsp
Worcestershire sauce a dash
Salt and freshly ground

black pepper
Potato 1, scrubbed and cut into chunky chips
Olive oil 1 tbsp
Balsamic vinegar 1 tbsp
Sunflower oil for greasing
Pork chop 1
Baby carrots and mangetout to serve, optional

Melt the butter in a medium-sized saucepan, add the onion and sugar and cook over a medium heat for 5–7 minutes, until the onion softens, but doesn't colour. Add the apple, sage and 4 tablespoons of water and cook over a gentle heat for 10–15 minutes, stirring it occasionally until it has softened to give a sauce. Add the Worcestershire sauce and season to taste.

Meanwhile, place the potato chips in a saucepan and cover with water, then place the pan on the hob and bring to the boil. Boil the potatoes for 5–7 minutes, then drain them well and tip into a bowl. Pour the olive oil and vinegar over the potatoes and season them with salt and pepper. Turn the chips to coat them in the oil, vinegar and seasoning.

Heat a ridged frying pan until hot and grease it lightly with the sunflower oil. Season the pork chop with salt and pepper and then add it to the pan and arrange the potato chips around the chop. Cook for 8–10 minutes on each side until the pork is cooked through, moving it to the edge of the pan if it starts to cook too quickly. Turn the chips regularly so they cook on all sides.

Serve the pork chop on the apple sauce and accompanied with the potato chips, baby carrots and mangetout.

Cook's tip
The pork chop and chunky chips may be cooked on an electric grill rather than on the hob. Reduce the cooking time.

Shopper's tip
If you're shopping in a supermarket, then look on the meat counter to buy individual pork chops.

Preparation time	**5 minutes**
Cooking time	**45 minutes**
Calories per portion	**863 Kcal**
Fat per portion	**37g**
of which saturated	**10.2g**
Serves	**1**

All-in-the-hole

Preheat the oven to 220°C/425°F/Gas 7. Place the red onion and sweet potato in a small gratin dish. Pour the olive oil over the vegetables and coat well. Place the sausages on top. Put the dish in the oven and bake for 15–20 minutes until they are a light golden colour, turning them occasionally so they cook evenly.

To make the batter, tip the flour into a bowl and whisk in the egg, milk, water, rosemary and seasoning. Pour the batter over the vegetables and sausages, and bake for 20–25 minutes, or until the batter has risen and is golden in colour, and is set when the dish is lightly shaken.

Serve immediately, as the batter will collapse quickly once the dish is removed from the oven.

Red onion 1, peeled and cut into thin wedges
Sweet potato 1, peeled and cut into chunks
Olive oil 1 tbsp
Reduced fat pork sausages 2 (approximately 150g/5oz)

For the batter
Plain flour 50g (2oz)
Egg 1
Milk 90ml (3fl oz)
Water 60ml (2fl oz)
Finely chopped rosemary ½ tbsp
Salt and black pepper

Cook's tip
For a more Mediterranean version, try using roast peppers and courgette in place of the onion and sweet potato.

Shopper's tip
To buy individual sausages with different combinations of flavour, visit a good butchers or a speciality sausage shop.

Preparation time | 20 minutes
Cooking time | 25–30 minutes
Calories per portion | 775 Kcal
Fat per portion | 41g
of which saturated | 11.9g
Serves | 1

Spicy chorizo pilaff

Olive oil 1 tbsp
Onion 1, peeled and chopped
Red pepper 1 very small, or half a large one, deseeded and cut into strips
Bacon 1 large rasher, de-rinded and cut into small strips
Long grain rice 50g (2oz)

Black olives 4–6
Sun-dried tomatoes 4 large, roughly chopped
Chicken stock 175ml (6fl oz)
Chorizo sausage 75g (3oz) piece, cut into thin slices

Heat the oil in a medium-sized, lidded frying pan. Add the onion and pepper and cook gently until softened, but not browned. Then add the bacon and stir until it just changes colour.

Stir the rice into the onion mixture. Add the olives, tomatoes and stock and bring to the boil, then reduce the heat, cover the pan with a lid and cook for 25 minutes, until the rice is cooked and all of the stock is absorbed.

Using a fork, gently mix the chorizo into the pilaff and allow it to heat through for 2–3 minutes. Serve immediately.

Cook's tip
When making a pilaff or risotto, ensure that the rice is evenly coated with oil before adding stock to prevent it becoming sticky.

Shopper's tip
Buy sun-dried tomatoes in smaller quantities from a deli counter or add olive oil to an opened jar. Store in the fridge.

Cook's tip

Store the unused half of lemon in a plastic bag in the fridge for up to 3–4 days. The juice of the lemon may be mixed with olive oil for a simple salad dressing.

Shopper's tip

Couscous is a wonderful store cupboard ingredient as it's so quick to prepare. It makes a great alternative to serving rice, pasta or mashed potatoes.

Preparation time	**5 minutes**
Marinating time	**15 minutes**
Cooking time	**10 minutes**
Calories per portion	**695 Kcal**
Fat per portion	**46g**
of which saturated	**17.4g**
Serves	**1**

Charmoula lamb chops with lemon couscous

For the charmoula coating
Ground coriander 1 tsp
Ground cumin 1 tsp
Ground cinnamon a pinch
Finely chopped coriander 1 tbsp
Finely chopped parsley 1 tbsp
Olive oil 1 tbsp
Garlic 1 clove, optional

For the lamb
Lamb cutlets 2
Sunflower oil for greasing

For the couscous
Couscous 75g (3oz)
Boiling water 90ml (3fl oz)
Lemon ½, grated zest and juice
Salt and freshly ground black pepper

Green salad to serve, optional

To make the charmoula coating (a traditional north African mixture) place the ground coriander, cumin and cinnamon, chopped coriander and parsley and the olive oil and garlic, if using, into the bowl of a mini-processor and whiz until smooth, or pound together using a pestle and mortar to give a smooth paste. Spread the paste over both sides of the lamb cutlets. Leave the lamb for at least 15 minutes to allow the flavours to marinate.

Heat a heavy based frying pan or ridged pan on a medium heat and grease it very lightly with sunflower oil. Add the lamb cutlets to the pan and cook for 3–5 minutes on each side, or until cooked to liking.

Put the couscous into a bowl and pour boiling water on top. Stir well, then leave it for about 4–5 minutes until all the water has been absorbed. Stir in the lemon zest and juice and season with salt and pepper.

Serve the chops on a bed of couscous and with a green salad.

Preparation time	5 minutes
Cooking time	35 minutes
Calories per portion	538 Kcal
Fat per portion	21g
of which saturated	9.4g
Serves	2

Suitable for vegetarians

Pea and bean risotto

Frozen peas 110g (4oz)
Butter 25g (1oz)
Hot vegetable stock 450ml (¾ pint)
Olive oil 1 tbsp
Small onion 1, peeled and chopped
Celery 2 sticks, chopped
Garlic 1 clove, peeled and chopped
Risotto rice 150g (5oz)

Dry white wine, sherry or vermouth
6 tbsp
Frozen soya beans or broad beans
50g (2oz)
Salt and freshly ground black pepper
Chopped flat parsley handful
Parmesan-like cheese shavings
2–3 tbsp made with a swivel-bladed peeler

Put half of the peas with 15g (½oz) of the butter and 3 tablespoons of the stock in a frying pan and cook gently for about 5 minutes, until tender. Spoon them onto a plate, mash with a fork and then set aside.

Heat the olive oil in the frying pan, add the onion, celery and garlic and fry over a low heat for about 4 minutes. Stir the rice into the pan and turn up the heat. Add the rest of the butter and when the rice grains are coated in it, add the wine, sherry or vermouth and stir until the bubbling stops.

Add about a third of the remaining stock and simmer the risotto. Keep stirring while adding stock every so often as it gets absorbed. After about 15 minutes cooking, taste the rice. It should still have a slight bite.

Add the rest of the stock, the mashed peas, the whole peas and the soya or broad beans. Taste and season well. Stir for a couple of minutes until the vegetables are heated through. Remove the pan from the heat, sprinkle with parsley and Parmesan shavings. Serve from the pan.

Cook's tip
If you don't want vegetarian risotto, dry fry Parma ham strips to put on the top, or griddle or fry fresh prawns or scallops.

Shopper's tip
Frozen vegetables are often higher in vitamins than 'fresh' ones, so keep a few varieties handy in your freezer.

Preparation time	10 minutes
Cooking time	20 minutes
Calories per portion	880 Kcal
Fat per portion	40g
of which saturated	19.4g
Serves	2
Suitable for vegetarians	

Pasta with spinach, blue cheese and pine nuts

Pasta shapes 225g (8oz)
Salt and freshly ground black pepper
Butter 15g (½oz)
Baby spinach 300g (11oz)
Blue cheese 110g (4oz)

Single cream 4 tbsp
Seedless raisins 45g (1½oz)
Ground nutmeg pinch
Pine nuts 25g (1oz), toasted

Bring a large saucepan of water to the boil and cook the pasta according to the manufacturer's instructions until 'al dente' – just cooked, but still slightly firm. Drain well, return to the pan and toss in the butter.

Meanwhile, wash the spinach thoroughly and remove any large stalks. Place in a clean saucepan while still wet, cover and cook over a medium heat for 4–5 minutes until wilted – the spinach will cook in the steam rising from the rinsing water. Drain well using a colander or sieve, pressing against the sides to squeeze out the excess liquid, then chop finely.

Crumble the cheese into small pieces and place in a saucepan with the cream and raisins. Heat gently until melted to a creamy sauce. Add the drained spinach, black pepper and ground nutmeg and stir well.

To serve, toss the pasta in the sauce and pile into warmed serving bowls and scatter the pine nuts over the top.

Cook's tip
If you have fresh spinach left over, rinse and shake it dry, then seal in a plastic bag. Keep in the fridge for up to 2 days.

Shopper's tip
If you like spinach, a more economical and convenient way to purchase this nutritious vegetable is in a frozen form.

Preparation time	10 minutes
Cooking time	40 minutes
Calories per portion	420 Kcal
Fat per portion	14g
of which saturated	2g
Serves	2

Perfect portions

Baked fish on a tray of vegetables

Baby potatoes 175g (6oz), scrubbed and thinly sliced
Small sweet potato 1, peeled and thinly sliced
Olive oil 2 tbsp
Salt and freshly ground black pepper
Red pepper 1, deseeded and cut into bite-sized pieces
Green pepper 1, deseeded and cut into bite-sized pieces
Courgette 1, trimmed and sliced
Cumin seeds ½ tsp, lightly crushed
Coriander seeds ½ tsp, lightly crushed
Firm white fish fillets 2 x 150g (5oz)
Small lemon 1, thinly sliced
Chopped coriander 2 tbsp

Cook's tip
You should be able to buy exact quantities of fish from your local fishmonger or fresh fish counter in the supermarket.

Preheat the oven to 200°C/400°F/Gas 6. Put the baby potato and sweet potato slices in a bowl and toss in 1 tablespoon of the olive oil. Season well. Arrange in a single layer on a small baking tray lined with greaseproof paper. Bake in the oven for 10 minutes.

Toss the peppers and courgette into the potato and drizzle with the remaining oil. Sprinkle with the seeds and bake for a further 10 minutes.

Wash and pat dry the fish. Season on the top and lay the fish over the vegetables with a few slices of lemon arranged on the top. Bake in the oven for 15–20 minutes, depending on thickness, until the fish is cooked through and the vegetables are tender. Drain and serve immediately, sprinkled with the chopped coriander.

Shopper's tip
For this recipe, choose white fish with a firm texture, like cod, ling, halibut or monkfish, so that it keeps its shape and doesn't break up.

Preparation time	**30 minutes**
Cooking time	**10 minutes**
Calories per portion	**597 Kcal**
Fat per portion	**36g**
of which saturated	**5g**
Serves	**2**

Artichoke and chicken salad

For the dressing
Olive oil 2 tbsp
Red wine vinegar 1 tbsp
Dijon mustard ½–1 tsp
Chopped parsley 2 tbsp
Finely shredded basil 2 tbsp

For the salad
Salad leaves such as oak leaf or lollo rosso, romaine lettuce and watercress
Avocado 1 small, stoned, peeled and cut into slices

Sunflower oil 1½ tbsp
Skinless chicken breast fillet 1 (approximately 200g/7oz), cut into thin strips
Red pepper 1, deseeded and cut into thin strips
Canned artichokes 4–6, drained and cut in half lengthways
Sun-dried tomatoes 75g (3oz), cut into thin strips
Marinated anchovy fillets 75g (3oz)

To make the dressing, put all the ingredients into a small bowl, whisk together and set aside. For the salad, arrange the salad leaves and sliced avocado on two serving plates.

Heat the sunflower oil in a large frying pan, add the chicken, red pepper strips, artichokes and sun-dried tomatoes and stir-fry for 2–3 minutes, until the chicken is just cooked and the pepper strips are slightly softened. Transfer the mixture onto the salad leaves, and add the anchovy fillets.

Pour the salad dressing into the frying pan, stir into the pan juices and heat for 1–2 minutes until very hot, but not boiling. Pour the dressing over the salad and serve immediately.

Cook's tip
Choose a ripe and ready-to-eat avocado or buy it 2–3 days before required and place in the fruit bowl next to bananas.

Shopper's tip
A small amount of marinated anchovies, red pepper strips or olives is more economical to buy from the deli counter.

Preparation time	**15 minutes**
Cooking time	**30 minutes**
Calories per portion	**545 Kcal**
Fat per portion	**25g**
of which saturated	**10g**
Serves	**2**

Cheesy chicken and leek gratin

Vegetable oil 1 tbsp
Leeks 2, trimmed, washed (see shopper's tip below) and sliced
Skinless chicken breast 1 (approx 200g/7oz), chopped
Ready-made white sauce 300ml (½ pint)
Snipped chives 2 tbsp
Salt and freshly ground

black pepper
French baton-style roll 1, thinly sliced
Wholegrain mustard 1 tbsp
Cheddar cheese 50g (2oz), grated

Heat the oil in a large saucepan and gently fry the leeks for 5 minutes until they are softened but not browned. Stir the chicken, white sauce and chives into the leeks and season lightly. Heat gently, stirring, for about 5 minutes until piping hot and the chicken is cooked.

Preheat the grill to hot. Arrange the bread slices on the grill rack and toast lightly for about a minute on each side until lightly brown. Transfer the chicken and leek sauce to a small, shallow, ovenproof baking dish.

Spread each of the toasted bread slices with mustard and then arrange on top of the chicken mixture, mustard-side up. Sprinkle with the cheese and place in the grill rack.

Cook under the grill for 3–4 minutes until the cheese is bubbling and golden on top. Serve immediately.

Cook's tip
If preferred, instead of the roll, use two slices of toasted white or granary bread and cut each into quarters.

Shopper's tip
Choose fresh green leeks with no signs of yellowing. Trim and slice lengthways, then rinse well under running water.

Preparation time	**5 minutes**
Cooking time	**15 minutes**
Calories per portion	**595 Kcal**
Fat per portion	**14g**
of which saturated	**2.4g**
Serves	**2**

Chicken with lemon and tarragon pasta

For the chicken
Olive oil 1–2 tbsp
Skinless chicken breast fillets 2
(approximately 200g (7oz) each),
halved horizontally
**Salt and freshly ground black
pepper**
Garlic 2 cloves, peeled and finely
chopped
Vine tomatoes 2, cut into wedges

For the pasta
Tagliatelle 150g (5oz)
Lemon juice to taste
Olive oil 1–2 tbsp
Tarrragon 15g pack, chopped

For the chicken, heat the oil in a ridged griddle (or frying pan) until
very hot. Season the chicken breasts, add to the griddle and cook
for 10–15 minutes, turning. Add the garlic and tomatoes for the
last minute or so.

Meanwhile, cook the pasta according to the packet's instructions,
then toss in the lemon juice, olive oil and tarragon.

Arrange the pasta in a neat pile on each plate. Cut the chicken
into strips and lay over the top with the vine tomatoes. Season
with salt and pepper.

Cook's tip
Store the leftover dried pasta in
an airtight jar and it will keep for
a long time.

Shopper's tip
Buy chicken breasts from the
butcher or fresh meat counter
at the supermarket – in that
way you will have exactly the
quantity and size you need.

Preparation time	**15 minutes**
Cooking time	**45 minutes**
Calories per portion	**840 Kcal**
Fat per portion	**48g**
of which saturated	**16.7g**
Serves	**2**

Spatchcock poussin with rice and green beans

Spatchcock poussin 2, weighing about 450g (1lb) each, ready seasoned if wished
Cajun seasoning 1 tsp
Butter 25g (1oz), chopped
Long grain rice 110g (4oz)

Chopped basil 1 tbsp
Chopped coriander 1 tbsp
Garlic 1 clove, peeled and finely chopped
Tomato 1, chopped
Sliced runner beans 190g pack

Preheat the oven to 190°C/375°F/Gas 5. Insert two skewers through the poussin so they cross each other. This keeps the bird flat during cooking. Arrange the poussin in a roasting tin. Sprinkle liberally with the cajun seasoning and dot with butter. Pop in the oven and cook for 40–45 minutes or until cooked through. Baste the poussin with the buttery juices once during cooking.

Meanwhile, cook the rice in a pan of boiling water according to the packet's instructions. Drain and rinse with boiling water and then drain again. Carefully stir in the chopped herbs, garlic and tomato.

Finally, cook the beans according to the pack's instructions. Arrange a mound of rice and a poussin on each plate, spooning over the buttery juices. Then add the green beans and serve immediately.

Cook's tip
Buy fresh herbs in pots and then you can take as much as you need and leave the rest growing on the windowsill.

Shopper's tip
If the poussin has not been spatchcocked, cut down the breastbone, open it out and then insert the skewers.

Preparation time	5 minutes
Cooking time	10–12 minutes
Calories per portion	989 Kcal
Fat per portion	55g
of which saturated	18.6g
Serves	2
Suitable for freezing	

Meat feast pizza

Pizza bases 1 pack of 2 thin and crispy
Bruschetta topping 270g jar
Cooked chicken tikka slices 130g pack
Pepperami 2 x 25g packs, sliced
Mozzarella 150g pack, drained and sliced
Basil leaves a handful

Preheat the oven to 220°C/425°F/Gas 7. Place the pizzas side by side on a clean work surface. Divide the bruschetta topping between the bases and spread to within 1cm (½in) of the edge of each pizza.

Scatter the chicken tikka slices, pepperami and mozzarella over the topping. Place the pizzas directly on the oven shelf with a baking sheet below to catch any juices and cook for 10–12 minutes or until the chicken is piping hot.

Garnish with fresh basil leaves and serve.

Cook's tip
As an altternative, try regular pizza topping and use any leftovers to add a extra flavour to tomato sauce.

Shopper's tip
You can get boxes of cooked chicken in all sorts of different flavours. Experiment with some of the others.

Preparation time	10 minutes
Cooking time	8 minutes
Calories per portion	357 Kcal
Fat per portion	17g
of which saturated	6.1g
Serves	2

Perfect portions

Gammon with tropical salsa

Gammon steaks 2 thick, about 200g (7oz) each
Vegetable oil for brushing
Clear honey 2 tsp

For the salsa
Pineapple chunks in pineapple juice 227g can, drained
Red onion 1 small, peeled and finely diced
Small chilli 1, deseeded and finely chopped, optional
Clear honey 1 tsp
Lime juice 2–3 tsp
Chopped coriander 2 tbsp
New potatoes and salad to serve, optional

Preheat the grill to hot. Snip the rind on the gammon steaks in 8–10 places. Brush the steaks lightly with oil and put them under the grill for 3 minutes, turn them and cook for another 3 minutes. Then turn them again and smooth the honey over the top and cook for 1 minute more. Put the meat on two plates and keep them warm.

While the meat is cooking, make the salsa. Dice the pineapple chunks and mix them with the red onion, chilli, if using, honey, the lime juice and coriander. Serve in a small bowl or straight on the gammon steaks together with new potatoes and a mixed salad.

Cook's tip
If you don't have a lime, use 1 teaspoon of soy sauce instead of the lime juice. It will give a stronger, less zesty flavour.

Shopper's tip
Canned pineapple is a useful storecupboard item for adding freshness to savoury dishes. Drink the juice.

Preparation time	**5 minutes**
Cooking time	**5 minutes**
Calories per portion	**845 Kcal**
Fat per portion	**67g**
of which saturated	**25.8g**
Serves	**2**

Pea, sun-blush tomato and Parma ham salad

Frozen peas 200g (7oz)
Sun-blush Mediterranean tomatoes in oil with garlic and oregano ½ a 240g tub, drained (reserve the oil) and roughly chopped
Parma ham 70g pack, slices cut into strips

Mozzarella 300g pack of 20 mini light balls, drained
Lemon ½, juice only
Salt and freshly ground black pepper
Rocket leaves to garnish

Cook the peas according to the packet's instructions, then drain and rinse in cold water. Tear the mozzarella into pieces. Arrange the peas on two plates and add the sun-blush tomatoes and then the Parma ham and mozzarella pieces.

Squeeze the lemon juice over the salad and drizzle with 4 tablespoons of the reserved oil. Add seasoning to taste and serve garnished with a few fresh rocket leaves.

Cook's tip
Use the leftover sun-blush tomatoes mixed with feta cheese on a crisp oven-baked potato.

Shopper's tip
Packs of fresh peas are the perfect size to make this salad in the summer. Out of season, use frozen peas.

Preparation time	**5 minutes**
Cooking time	**10 minutes**
Calories per portion	**348 Kcal**
Fat per portion	**12g**
of which saturated	**2.3g**
Serves	**2**

Saucy pork with cabbage

Vegetable oil 1 tbsp
Lean, boneless pork 225g (8oz), cut into thin strips
Leek 1, trimmed, washed and shredded
Eating apple 1, cored and thinly sliced
Small Savoy cabbage ½, cored and shredded
Worcestershire sauce 2 tbsp
Clear honey 2 tsp
Salt and freshly ground black pepper
Cooked rice to serve, optional

Heat the oil in a wok or large frying pan until hot and stir-fry the pork for about 3 minutes until browned all over. Add the leek, apple and cabbage and continue to stir-fry for a further 2 minutes until well coated in the oil and pork juices.

Add the Worcestershire sauce and stir-fry for a further 2 minutes until the vegetables are tender. Add the honey and season to taste. Serve immediately with freshly cooked rice.

Cook's tip
Wrap the remaining half of cabbage in cling film and keep in the fridge. Use within 3 days for a crunchy coleslaw.

Shopper's tip
This recipe also works well with red cabbage, although it will require longer cooking as it has denser flesh.

Preparation time	5 minutes
Cooking time	10 minutes
Calories per portion	596 Kcal
Fat per portion	21g
of which saturated	4.6g
Serves	2

Stir-fried sticky pork with chilli

Toasted sesame oil 2 tbsp
Boneless loin pork steaks 2, with fat removed and cut into thin strips
Stir-fry mix 220g pack containing vegetables such as red onion, Chinese broccoli, red pepper and spinach
Fresh egg noodles 350g pack
Sweet chilli dipping sauce 2–3 tbsp

Heat the oil in a wok until it is very hot, add the strips of pork and stir-fry for about 3 minutes.

Add the pack of stir-fry vegetables and continue stir-frying for another 2–3 minutes or until the spinach starts to wilt.

Add the noodles with the chilli sauce and cook for a further 3 minutes or until everything is tender and cooked.

Cook's tip
It is well worth buying a wok to make stir-fries – the results are so much better.

Shopper's tip
See the Shopper's tip on page 77 for information on where to buy toasted sesame oil. If unavailable, use plain sesame oil.

Cook's tip

To cook spinach on a hob, pop it in a non-stick frying pan with a knob of butter and cook, tossing with a spoon until the spinach is just wilted.

Shopper's tip

Learn to enjoy picking up food as you need it. Select the potatoes from the help yourself section and the lamb from the butcher's counter.

Preparation time	**20 minutes**
Cooking time	**30 minutes**
Calories per portion	**757 Kcal**
Fat per portion	**52g**
of which saturated	**21.9g**
Serves	**2**

Rack of lamb with garlic mash and spinach

Rack of lamb 1x 6
Salt and freshly ground black pepper
Redcurrant jelly 1 tbsp
Dried rosemary 1 tsp
Potatoes 2 large, peeled and roughly chopped
Garlic 1–2 cloves

Olive oil 2–3 tbsp
Baby spinach 180g pack, washed and trimmed

For the gravy
Redcurrant jelly 2 tsp
Lamb stock 150ml (¼ pint)

Preheat the oven to 200ºC/400ºF/Gas 6. Season the rack of lamb with salt and pepper and place in a roasting tin. Spoon the redcurrant jelly and rosemary into a bowl and heat in the microwave on full power for about 30 seconds or until the mixture has melted.

Brush the redcurrant jelly mix over the fat side of the rack of lamb and cook in the preheated oven for 25–30 minutes. The time the lamb takes to cook will depend on how pink you like your lamb and how much meat is on the rack. See the table on page 9.

Meanwhile, cook the potatoes in a saucepan of boiling water until tender. Drain well. Put the garlic cloves and 2 tablespoons of the olive oil in a processor and whiz to chop the garlic. Add the hot potatoes and plenty of pepper and, using the pulse button, whiz the potatoes to a smooth mash. Add the extra oil if needed.

Remove the lamb from the oven and transfer to warmed plates. Make the gravy by adding the redcurrant jelly to the pan juices and add the lamb stock. Boil for 2 minutes, stirring and scraping up bits from the base of the pan.

Pierce the spinach in the bag and cook on high in the microwave for 2½ minutes or according to the pack's instructions. Carefully open the bag, drain the spinach and stir into the mash. Carve the lamb and serve the cutlets with a pile of the spinach mash together with the gravy.

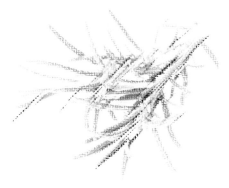

Preparation time	10 minutes
Cooking time	45 minutes
Calories per portion	418 Kcal
Fat per portion	21g
of which saturated	8.5g
Serves	2

Lancashire hotpot chops

Lean, boneless lamb chops
2, trimmed
Salt and freshly ground black pepper
Dried rosemary 1 tsp
Onion 1 small, peeled and thinly sliced

Carrot 1 small, peeled and thinly sliced
Potato 1 small, peeled and thinly sliced
Olive oil 2 tsp
Fresh rosemary to garnish

Preheat the oven to 180°C/350°F/Gas 4. Wash and pat dry the chops and season on both sides. Place in a small roasting tin lined with greaseproof paper, and sprinkle with a little of the rosemary.

Arrange alternate layers of onion, carrot and potato on top of each chop. Season and sprinkle with remaining rosemary. Drizzle with the oil and bake in the oven for 40–45 minutes until tender and cooked through. If the potatoes are not golden enough, brown under the grill.

To serve, drain the lamb and garnish with the fresh rosemary.

Cook's tip
To make the most of the oven heat, bake sliced courgettes and peppers in a little stock alongside the lamb.

Shopper's tip
Boneless loin chops make a good choice for this recipe. It works equally well with pork chops.

Preparation time | 10 minutes
Cooking time | 5 minutes
Calories per portion | 299 Kcal
Fat per portion | 5g
of which saturated | 1.5g
Serves | 2

Perfect portions

Beef noodle pot

Hot vegetable or beef stock
750–900ml (1¼–1½ pints)
Root ginger 2.5cm (1in) piece, peeled and cut into fine slivers
Garlic 1 clove, peeled and cut into fine slivers
Soy sauce 2 tbsp
Mushrooms 4 cup or 6 button, wiped and thinly sliced
Sweetcorn (canned or frozen) 4 rounded tbsp
Stir-fry beef strips or a small lean steak thinly sliced 150–175g (5–6oz)
Medium 'straight-to-wok' noodles 150g pack
Spring onions 2, trimmed, washed and thinly sliced
Pak choi 2 small heads, halved or quartered
Chilli 1, deseeded and finely shredded, optional

Pour the stock into a large saucepan and add the ginger, garlic and soy sauce. Bring just to the boil.

Add the mushrooms then bring back to the boil and add the sweetcorn. Stir the beef strips into the stock then add the noodles and spring onions. Place the pak choi on top so that they steam cook for 2 minutes.

Use a draining spoon to divide the meat, noodles and vegetables between two large hot bowls, then ladle the stock over. Garnish with slivers of chilli, if using. Eat using chopsticks, then a soup spoon or a spoon and fork.

Cook's tip
If you like Thai-style food, add lemongrass and lime leaves to the stock and use fish sauce and more lime juice.

Shopper's tip
'Straight-to-wok' noodles are very easy to use and come in 2 x 150g packs. They keep well in the store cupboard.

Make now, eat later

Whether you're popping out to a dance class, partying or patting down the cushions before a game of cards, you might not have time to prepare a satisfying supper.

The solution is another 'P': preparation. All these meals can be created well in advance and will just require the finishing touches before you sit down, put your feet up and enjoy good food.

With such a variety of choice, you'll be far less tempted to ring for a take away as these recipes are tasty and can be finished in minutes.

Preparation time	**5 minutes**
Cooking time	**30 minutes**
Calories per portion	**641 Kcal**
Fat per portion	**28g**
of which saturated	**14.3g**
Serves	**1**

Suitable for vegetarians + freezing

Cheese and tomato gratin

White sliced bread 3–4 slices, buttered and crusts removed
Tomatoes 2, sliced
Gruyère cheese 50g (2oz), grated
Egg 1
Milk 150ml (¼ pint)
Salt and freshly ground black pepper

Cut the slices of bread diagonally into four and arrange them in a 600ml (1 pint), buttered ovenproof dish. Arrange the tomato slices over the top, pushing some of them between the slices of bread. Sprinkle the cheese over the top, pushing some of it between the slices of bread.

Lightly beat together the egg and milk and pour the mixture over the bread. Season with salt and pepper. Cover the dish and chill for 2–3 hours, or overnight.

Preheat the oven to 180°C/350°F/Gas 4. Uncover the dish, then bake the cheese gratin in the centre of the oven for 20–30 minutes, or until it is a light golden colour. Remove it from the oven and serve immediately.

Cook's tip
You don't need fresh bread for this recipe, it works better with dry bread, so it's ideal for using up stale leftovers.

Shopper's tip
Look out for half-loaves, to save buying a full loaf. The slice sizes are the same, but the loaves are a shorter length.

Preparation time	10 minutes
Marinating time	2–3 days
Cooking time	20 minutes
Calories per portion	693 Kcal
Fat per portion	51g
of which saturated	7.6g
Serves	1

Marinated kippers with potato and beetroot salad

For the kipper
Kipper 1, filleted
Crushed coriander seeds 1 tsp
Shallot 1, peeled and thinly sliced
Bay leaf 1
Lemon 1, grated zest and juice
Olive oil 4 tbsp
Wholegrain mustard 1 tsp
Salt and freshly ground black pepper
Mixed salad leaves to serve

For the potato salad
New potatoes 4–5, scrubbed
Spring onions 2, trimmed, washed and sliced
Chopped dill 1 tbsp
Light mayonnaise 2 tbsp
Shredded beetroot 1 tbsp from a jar, drained

For the kipper, place the fillet in a dish and sprinkle with the coriander seeds. Add the shallot, bay leaf and lemon zest. Whisk together the lemon juice, olive oil and mustard and pour it over the fish. Season with black pepper.

Cover the dish and chill the kipper in the fridge for at least 2–3 days before eating it, turning the fillets and shallots daily so that they are thoroughly coated in the dressing.

For the potato salad, cook the potatoes in boiling water for about 15–18 minutes or until they are just tender. Then drain them and rinse under cold running water to cool them quickly and then slice them.

Mix the sliced potato, spring onion and dill into the mayonnaise with the beetroot and season with salt and pepper. Cover the bowl and keep the potato salad chilled until serving. Remove the potato salad from the fridge at least 15 minutes before serving so that it comes to room temperature. Scatter the salad leaves into a plate and spoon over the potato salad. Drain the fish fillet from the excess oil and serve it on top.

Cook's tip
Marinate the kipper 2–3 days in advance of eating for the flavour to develop. Make potato salad up to 24 hours before serving.

Shopper's tip
It may seem like a lot of olive oil in the recipe for just one serving, but there needs to be sufficient to cover the fish.

Preparation time	10 minutes
Chilling time	3–8 hours
Cooking time	5 minutes
Calories per portion	422 Kcal
Fat per portion	14g
of which saturated	3.1g
Serves	1

Salmon with couscous, peas and cucumber

Couscous 50g (2oz)
Boiling water 60ml (2fl oz)
Snipped chives 2 tbsp
Peas 50g (2oz), cooked and drained
Cucumber 5cm (2in) piece, deseeded and chopped

Olive oil 1 tsp
Salt and freshly ground black pepper
Lime 1, juice only
Ready-to-eat honey roast salmon flakes 135g pack

Tip the couscous into a bowl and add the boiling water, cover with cling film and leave to stand for 5 minutes or until the water is absorbed (or according to the packet's instructions). Fluff up the couscous with a fork. Add the chives, peas, cucumber and oil, and mix well. Season to taste with salt and pepper. Leave to cool.

Cover with cling film and chill for a minimum of 3 hours or up to 8 hours. Just before serving, stir in the lime juice to taste and the salmon flakes. Mix well, spoon into a bowl and enjoy.

Cook's tip
To serve as a side dish, replace the salmon flakes with one tomato, very finely chopped.

Shopper's tip
You don't have to buy a whole or even half a cucumber. Look out for handy size chunks sold as portions of cucumber.

Stuffed chicken breast

Preparation time	**30 minutes**
Cooking time	**15–20 minutes**
Calories per portion	**754 Kcal**
Fat per portion	**48g**
of which saturated	**17.1g**
Serves	**1**
Suitable for freezing	

Skinless chicken breast fillet 1 (approximately 200g/7oz)
Butter 25g (1oz) softened
Mixed dried herbs ½–1 tsp
Sun-dried tomatoes 4 large
Basil leaves 4–6

Plain flour 1 tbsp
Egg 1, beaten
White breadcrumbs 25g (1oz)
Sunflower oil 2 tbsp
Green salad to serve, optional

Place the chicken breast between two sheets of cling film and beat it out to about 5mm (¼in) thick with a meat mallet or a rolling pin.

In a small bowl, blend together the butter and dried herbs. Remove the cling film from the chicken, and place it, skinned-side down, on a board.

Spread the softened butter along the centre of the chicken breast, and then place the sun-dried tomatoes, slightly overlapping, in a line on top of the butter. Cover the tomatoes with basil leaves.

Fold each end of the chicken breast in and over the filling, then fold in the sides and secure with cocktail sticks. Lightly flour the chicken, shaking off any excess, then coat with the beaten egg, and then with the breadcrumbs.

Heat the oil in a small frying pan, add the coated chicken and cook gently, turning occasionally, until golden brown and the chicken is cooked through – about 10–15 minutes. Drain on kitchen paper, carefully remove the cocktail sticks and serve hot with a crisp green salad.

Cook's tip
The chicken breast can be prepared the night before or earlier in the day, and be kept, covered, in the refrigerator.

Shopper's tip
A coffee grinder is perfect for making a small amount of breadcrumbs. Fresh breadcrumbs freeze well.

Preparation time	**10 minutes**
Chilling time	**3–8 hours**
Cooking time	**16 minutes**
Calories per portion	**689 Kcal**
Fat per portion	**34g**
of which saturated	**11.7g**
Serves	**1**

Thai beef salad

Heat the oil in a frying pan and cook the steak for 2–3 minutes on each side, turning once. The exact time will depend on the thickness of the meat, but try to keep it medium rare. Transfer to a dish.

Add the shallot, chilli and garlic and the fish and soy sauces to the pan and leave to simmer for 2 minutes. Pour the juices over the sirloin, add the lime juice and sugar and turn the steak so it is coated in the marinade. Leave to cool, then cover with cling film and chill for a minimum of 3 hours or up to 8 hours.

Cook the rice according to the packet's instructions and set a pile on a plate. Thinly slice the steak and pop on top. Drizzle with the marinade and garnish with coriander and thing carrot ribbons made using a swivel bladed vegetable peeler.

Toasted sesame oil 1 tbsp
Sirloin steak 1 (about 175g/6oz)
Shallot 1, peeled and finely sliced
Chilli 1, deseeded and finely chopped
Garlic 1 clove, peeled and finely chopped

Fish sauce 1 tbsp
Soy sauce 1 tbsp
Lime 1, juice only
Soft brown sugar 1 tsp
Long grain white rice 50g (2oz)
Coriander sprigs to garnish
Small carrot to garnish

Cook's tip
Use leftover fish sauce and toasted sesame oil to add extra flavour to stir-fries.

Shopper's tip
You can find toasted sesame oil next to the fish sauce on the Oriental shelf of most supermarkets.

Preparation time	**20 minutes**
Cooking time	**30 minutes**
Calories per portion	**557 Kcal**
Fat per portion	**42g**
of which saturated	**30.6g**
Serves	**2**

Suitable for vegetarians + freezing

Mixed vegetable korma

Sunflower oil 1 tbsp
Onion 1, peeled and roughly chopped
Curry powder 2 tsp
Aubergine 225g (8oz), cut into thick slices, then into quarters
Fine green beans 75g (3oz), trimmed and cut into short pieces
Red pepper 110g (4oz) piece, deseeded and cut into strips

Courgette 1, trimmed and sliced
New potatoes 175–225g (6–8oz) small, washed and cut into quarters or slices, depending on size
Vegetable stock 225ml (8fl oz)
Coconut cream 200ml carton
Coriander a few sprigs, to garnish, optional
Naan bread to serve, optional

Heat the oil in a large saucepan, add the onion and cook gently until it has softened but not browned.

Stir the curry powder into the onion, add all the remaining vegetables and mix together gently. Add the stock and bring up to the boil, then reduce the heat, cover the pan with a tight-fitting lid and cook gently for 25–30 minutes until the vegetables are just cooked through – take care not to over cook the vegetables, as they may break up when reheated.

Allow the curry to cool, then refrigerate until you are ready to serve it later in the day – or even the next day.

When ready to serve, stir the coconut cream into the vegetables and reheat gently until piping hot. Serve sprinkled with the coriander and accompanied with torn pieces of warm naan bread.

Preparation time	10 minutes
Cooking time	30 minutes
Calories per portion	614 Kcal
Fat per portion	41g
of which saturated	20.8g
Serves	2

Suitable for vegetarians + freezing

Two cheese and onion tart

Ready-rolled puff pastry 1 sheet from a 425g pack
Tomato chutney or ketchup 2 tbsp
Onion 1 small, peeled and thinly sliced
Baby plum or cherry tomatoes 6, halved

Cheddar cheese, Double Gloucester or Red Leicester mixed with a blue cheese like Gorgonzola or Stilton 110g (4oz), cut into cubes
Freshly ground black pepper
Chopped parsley to garnish

Preheat the oven to 220°C/425°F/Gas 7. Carefully unroll the whole pack of pastry and put one sheet (measuring 23 x 28cm /9 x 11in) on to a heavy baking sheet. Re-roll and re-wrap the other sheet and chill or freeze for later use.

With a sharp knife, mark a border about 1.5cm (½in) in from the edge all round and lightly mark it for decoration. With a fork, prick inside the border, to keep the pastry flat while it cooks.

Spread the chutney or ketchup inside the border, then scatter the onion slices over the sauce, followed by the cheese cubes and tomato halves Season with pepper.

Bake the tart in the bottom half of the oven for about 30 minutes until the pastry is browned and crispy. Cool for a few minutes and then sprinkle with a little parsley. Serve the tart warm or cold.

Cook's tip
This is easy to assemble and can be left in the fridge, loosely covered with cling film, ready for baking when you want to.

Shopper's tip
Ready-rolled pastry is a good stand-by as it thaws quickly for a speedy base for savoury and sweet tarts.

Preparation time	10 minutes
Cooking time	40 minutes
Cooling time	10 minutes
Calories per portion	414 Kcal
Fat per portion	17g
of which saturated	4.1g
Serves	2
Suitable for vegetarians	

Roasted vegetable pasta

Preheat the oven to 200°C/400°F/Gas 6. Mix the onion wedges, chunks of courgette, strips of pepper and the garlic clove(s) in a roasting tin with the oil, coating the vegetables. Roast for 35 minutes, stirring halfway through cooking. Add the tomatoes and cook another 5 minutes. Carefully spoon into a shallow dish and leave, loosely covered, to cool.

When you are ready to eat this dish, cook the pasta in a large pan, according to the packet's instructions. Meanwhile, slip the cooked garlic from the roasted vegetables out of its skin and microwave the vegetables on high power for about 3 minutes until piping hot. (If you don't have a microwave, reheat the vegetables gently in the pan, then add the pasta.)

Drain the pasta, add the garlic to the pan and squash it down, with a little extra oil then put the pasta back in and gently stir in the hot vegetables. Season well with salt and pepper and add the basil leaves, whole or torn. Serve from the pan sprinkled with Parmesan cheese.

Red onion 1, unpeeled, cut into thin wedges
Courgettes 2, trimmed and cut into small chunks
Yellow or red pepper 1, deseeded and cut into strips
Garlic 1–2 cloves, unpeeled
Olive oil 2 tbsp

Baby plum tomatoes 12
Fusilli or other short pasta 110g (4oz)
Salt and freshly ground black pepper
Basil leaves handful
Grated Parmesan-like cheese 3–4 tbsp

Cook's tip
You can cook the full quantity of vegetables up to a few days in advance and keep them in the fridge.

Shopper's tip
Pasta is great for a quick meal. Buy in-season vegetables on the market and roast a whole batch of them.

Cook's tip
Cooked rice freezes well, so it's worth boiling or steaming a batch and freezing in handy portion packs.

Shopper's tip
Sweet potatoes have a more moist flavour and texture than usual white-fleshed potatoes, but you can use them instead if you prefer – you will probably need to add beaten egg in order to bind together the mixture.

Preparation time	30 minutes
Chilling time	1 hour
Cooking time	20 minutes
Calories per portion	497 Kcal
Fat per portion	13g
of which saturated	2.1g
Serves	2
Suitable for freezing	

Tuna, rice and sweet potato fish cakes

Sweet potato 1 large, peeled and cut into small pieces
Brown or white rice 75g (3oz)
Spring onions 2, trimmed, washed and finely sliced
Tuna in brine 198g can, drained and flaked

Smoked paprika large pinch
Salt and freshly ground black pepper
Plain flour 2 tbsp
Sunflower oil 2 tbsp

Place the potato pieces in a large saucepan and cover with water. Bring to the boil and cook for 10–12 minutes until tender and cooked through. Drain well, return to the pan, mash until smooth and set aside to cool.

Cook the rice according to the packet's instructions. Drain and rinse well with cold water until the rice is cool. Then stir into the mashed potato along with the spring onion, tuna and smoked paprika. Season well.

Divide the mixture into eight and form into 7cm (3in) fish cakes. Place on a plate lined with greaseproof paper, cover and chill for at least 1 hour or until required.

To cook, lightly dust the fish cakes with flour on both sides. Heat the oil in a frying pan until hot and cook the cakes for 5–8 minutes on each side, carefully turning with a palette knife, until golden and hot. Drain and serve immediately.

Preparation time	**5 minutes**
Cooking time	**1 hour 20 minutes**
Calories per portion	**443 Kcal**
Fat per portion	**22g**
of which saturated	**7.7g**
Serves	**2**
Suitable for freezing	

Shanghai-style spare ribs

Pork spare ribs 6 good size meaty ribs, about 680g (1½lb)
Spring onions 2, trimmed and washed
Root ginger piece about 2.5cm (1in) square, peeled and sliced

Sugar 3 tbsp
Dry sherry 3 tbsp
Soy sauce 3 tbsp
Coleslaw to serve, optional
Sweetcorn, tomato and red onion salad to serve, optional

Put the spare ribs in a saucepan big enough to sit them comfortably in one layer. Add the spring onions, whole, and the ginger, along with the sugar, sherry and soy sauce and 600ml (1 pint) water. The liquid should cover the ribs well.

Bring to the boil, put the lid on the pan and turn the heat down to low and leave to simmer for 45 minutes. Turn off the heat and leave the ribs in the pan until later in the day when you want to cook them.

From cold, bring the pan to the boil then take the lid off, remove the spring onions and pieces of ginger and cook the ribs on a high heat for 25–30 minutes until the liquid is thick and syrupy and coating the ribs. Do watch the ribs for the last 10 minutes and keep turning them so they are well coated but do not stick to the pan. Serve the ribs with coleslaw and a sweetcorn, diced tomato and red onion salad – they make a lovely sticky treat, so have a finger bowl or serviette handy.

Cook's tip
Make the whole recipe and keep what you don't eat in the fridge for a couple of days or freeze them for longer.

Shopper's tip
Buy spare ribs in packs or loose from the supermarket meat counter. Get them when on special offer as they freeze well.

Preparation time	**15 minutes**
Cooking time	**15 minutes**
Calories per portion	**486 Kcal**
Fat per portion	**30g**
of which saturated	**14g**
Serves	**2**

Italian mushroom bake

Beefsteak tomato 1 large
Salt and freshly ground black pepper
Basil leaves 6–8, plus extra to garnish
Flat chestnut mushrooms 4 large, wiped and stalks removed if necessary
Vegetable oil for brushing
Salami 4 slices, optional
Ham 2 slices, approximately 50g (2oz) each
Mozzarella 195g pack, drained and thinly sliced
Wholemeal bread 4 thick slices
Black or stuffed green olives to garnish, optional

Using a small, sharp, pointed knife, remove the core-end of the tomato and cut a very thin slice from the bottom – to make it level. Then cut the tomato into four thick slices.

Line a baking tray with non-stick foil. Place the tomato slices on the foil, season well and then cover them with the basil leaves. Place the mushrooms on top of the basil, brush lightly with oil, season well and then add the slices of salami, if using, and ham, followed by the mozzarella. Cover with cling film and store in the fridge for up to 3 hours until you are ready to eat.

When you are ready to eat, preheat the oven to 200°C/400°F/Gas 6. Cook the prepared toppings on a baking sheet in the centre of the oven for 15 minutes until the mushrooms are just cooked, and the cheese is melted and browned.

Toast the bread and place on two serving plates. Using a large fish slice, carefully transfer each tomato stack onto the toast. Garnish with olives, if using, and serve immediately, scattered with basil leaves.

Cook's tip
To clean the mushrooms, wipe them with kitchen paper or with a mushroom brush – do not wash them.

Shopper's tip
Salami comes in many guises; look for packets with a mixture of types so you can experiment with different flavours.

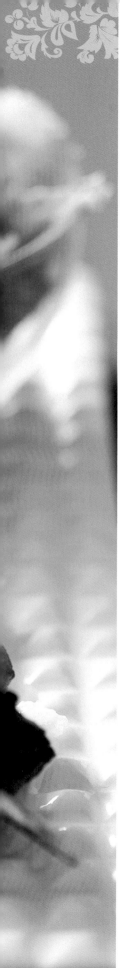

Preparation time	15 minutes
Marinating and soaking	1 hour
Cooking time	12 minutes
Calories per portion	311 Kcal
Fat per portion	13g
of which saturated	5.4g
Serves	2
Suitable for freezing	

Curried lamb and apricot skewers

Lean boneless lamb 225g (8oz), trimmed
Natural yogurt 3 tbsp
Mild curry paste 2 tsp
Tomato purée 1 tsp
Garlic 1 clove, peeled and crushed
Salt and freshly ground black pepper

Dried apricots 12
Boiling water approximately 225ml (8fl oz)
Vegetable oil 1 tsp
Chopped coriander 2 tbsp
Rice to serve, optional
Green salad to serve, optional

Cut the lamb into 2cm (¾in) thick pieces and place in a small bowl. Mix the yogurt with the curry paste, tomato purée and garlic, and toss into the lamb. Season lightly, cover and chill for at least an hour, or until required.

Put the apricots in a small heatproof bowl and just cover with boiling water. Set aside for at least 30 minutes, or until required.

To cook, drain the apricots and pat dry with kitchen paper. Preheat the grill to medium. Thread a few pieces of lamb with three apricots on each of four skewers, then place on a grill rack. Mix any remaining yogurt marinade with the oil and brush lightly over the lamb and apricots. Cook for 5–6 minutes on each side, basting with marinade occasionally, until cooked through. Drain and serve immediately on a bed of rice, if using, sprinkled with chopped coriander. Accompany with a crisp salad.

Cook's tip
Using yogurt in a marinade keeps meat moist during cooking. This combination also works well with chicken.

Shopper's tip
Check out boneless lamb chops; you may find they make an exact quantity rather than having to buy larger cuts.

Make the most of...

This clever chapter allows you to make the most of buying in larger quantities – which are often cheaper – while giving you a choice of what you would like to cook.

Simply buy the main ingredient and then choose which two of the three recipes you would like to try. Each recipe is quite different so that it won't be, 'Not chicken again,' but rather, 'Great, after yesterday's roast chicken, a lemony chicken soup is just what I need.'

If you're cooking for one, you might want to freeze the extra portion to enjoy another time.

Preparation time	10 minutes
Cooking time	15 minutes
Calories per portion	385 Kcal
Fat per portion	22g
of which saturated	3.1g
Serves	2
Suitable for vegetarians + freezing	

. . . . . . canned beans

To make two of the following three recipes, you will need to buy a 410g can of beans, such as kidney beans, pinto or butterbeans. You will need half the can for each recipe.

Beany burgers

Vegetable oil 3 tbsp
Onion 1 small, peeled and chopped
Canned beans ½ x 410g can, drained and rinsed
Cooked broad beans 50g (2oz)
Carrot 1 small, peeled and grated
Yeast extract ½ tsp
Wholemeal breadcrumbs
50g (2oz)
Egg yolk 1, beaten
Wholemeal flour 1 tbsp
Large wholemeal buns 2, split and toasted
Tomatoes, red onion and lettuce leaves to serve, optional
Chunky chips to serve, optional

1. Heat 2 teaspoons of the oil in a small frying pan and gently fry the onion for 5 minutes until just softened. Set aside to cool.

2. Put the canned beans and cooked broad beans in a liquidiser and whiz until mashed together. Transfer to a bowl and add the carrot, yeast extract and cooked onion. Stir in the breadcrumbs and bind together with the egg yolk.

3. Divide the mixture into two and, using wet hands, form into burgers. Lightly dust both sides with the flour.

4. Heat the remaining oil in a frying pan and gently fry the burgers for 3–4 minutes on each side, turning with a palette knife, until golden and hot. Drain and serve immediately in a toasted bun with some lettuce leaves. Top with slices of tomato and red onion, accompanied with chunky chips on the side.

Cook's tip
You can grill the burgers in a foil-lined grill tray under a medium setting. Brush with a little oil and cook for 4 minutes each side.

Shopper's tip
These burgers are seasoned with yeast extract, which is quite savoury so you won't need to add any more flavouring.

Preparation time	10 minutes
Cooking time	10 minutes
Calories per portion	381 Kcal
Fat per portion	18g
of which saturated	6.8g
Serves	2

Suitable for vegetarians + freezing

...... canned beans
Mexican-style pizza

Onion 1 small, peeled and chopped
Tomatoes 2, chopped
Garlic 1 clove, peeled and crushed
Canned beans ½ x 410g can, drained and rinsed
Olive oil 1 tbsp
Chilli powder ½ tsp
Coriander small bunch, chopped
Salt and freshly ground black pepper
Flour tortillas 2
Cheddar cheese 50g (2oz), grated
Rocket 2 handfuls
Lime ½, cut into wedges, to serve

Preheat the oven to 200°C/400°F/Gas 6. In a small bowl, mix together the onion, tomatoes, garlic, beans, oil, chilli powder, coriander and plenty of seasoning.

Arrange the tortillas on a large baking sheet lined with greaseproof paper and spoon the tomato and bean mixture onto each tortilla. Sprinkle each with cheese and bake for about 10 minutes until golden and bubbling.

Serve immediately, each with a topping of rocket leaves and with wedges of lime to squeeze over.

Cook's tip
Flour tortillas usually come in multi-packs. To freeze, interlace each tortilla in a stack with greaseproof paper or freezer sheets and seal in a freezer bag.

Shopper's tip
For a cheat's version, buy ready-made fresh tomato salsa and mix with leftover beans.

Cook's tip

For a vegetarian version, replace the tuna with an equal quantity of diced mozzarella. Add a few halved cherry tomatoes for extra colour.

Shopper's tip

For a richer salad, use well-drained tuna canned in sunflower oil.

Preparation time	10 minutes
Cooling time	40 minutes
Cooking time	5 minutes
Calories per portion	427 Kcal
Fat per portion	25g
of which saturated	3.6g
Serves	2

...... canned beans
Tonno e fagioli

Green beans 150g (5oz), topped, tailed and halved
Frozen broad beans 150g (5oz), skinned, or frozen soya beans
Canned beans ½ x 410g can, drained and rinsed
Tuna 198g can, drained and flaked

Red onion 1 small, peeled and finely chopped
Parsley small bunch, chopped
Capers 2 tbsp, drained
Salt and freshly ground black pepper
Vinaigrette-style salad dressing 4 tbsp

Bring a small saucepan of water to the boil and add the green and broad beans. Bring back to the boil, cover and cook for 4–5 minutes until just tender. Drain well and rinse in cold water to cool. Set aside for about 40 minutes to cool completely.

Meanwhile, put the canned beans in a bowl and gently mix the tuna, onion, parsley and capers into the beans. Lightly season and then cover and chill until required.

To serve, mix the cold green and broad beans into the tuna mixture and gently toss in the salad dressing. Pile on to plates and serve.

Preparation time	15 minutes
Cooling time	20 minutes
Cooking time	45 minutes
Calories per portion	1072 Kcal
Fat per portion	58g
of which saturated	27.6g
Serves	2
Suitable for freezing	

. . . . . . puff pastry

To make two of the following three recipes, you will need to buy one 500g pack of puff pastry, available in the chiller section of the supermarket. You will need half the packet for each recipe.

Chicken and leek pie

Butter 50g (2oz)
Baby leek 1, trimmed, washed and sliced
Carrots 2, peeled and thickly sliced
Skinless chicken breasts 2 (approximately 200g (7oz) each), chopped

Plain flour 2 tbsp
Milk 350ml (12fl oz)
Chicken stock cube 1
Salt and freshly ground black pepper
Puff pastry ½ x 500g pack
Egg 1, beaten for glaze

1   Preheat the oven to 200°C/400°F/Gas 6. Melt half of the butter in a saucepan and add the leek and carrots and cook for 7–10 minutes, until the vegetables have softened. Remove from the pan and place in a 900ml (1½ pint) pie dish. Add the chicken to the pan and cook over a high heat for 3–4 minutes, turning the meat occasionally until browned. Add the meat to the pie dish and mix with the vegetables.

2   Melt the remaining butter in the pan. Add the flour and stir for a minute, then gradually add the milk, allowing the mixture to come to the boil between each addition and beating well. Add the stock cube and seasoning and stir until dissolved. Pour the sauce over the chicken and vegetables. Leave the filling to cool for 15–20 minutes.

3   Roll out the pastry on a lightly floured surface, until slightly larger than the pie dish. Cut thin strips off the edges, dampen the dish rim with water and stick on the strips. Dampen the pastry around the rim and place the main piece of pastry on top. Trim off excess and seal the edges with a fork. Brush egg glaze over the pastry and make a couple of holes in the centre.

4   Place the dish on a baking tray and bake for 25–30 minutes, or until the pastry is golden. Serve immediately.

Cook's tip
Freeze when the pie has been covered with pastry. Allow the pie to defrost thoroughly before baking in the oven.

Shopper's tip
If you can't buy an individual leek, then an onion may be substituted in its place.

Preparation time	**10 minutes**
Cooking time	**40 minutes**
Calories per pasty	**735 Kcal**
Fat per pasty	**50g**
of which saturated	**19.9g**
Serves	**2**
Suitable for freezing	

...... *puff pastry*
Cheese and bacon pasties

Preheat the oven to 220°C/425°F/Gas 7. Heat the sunflower oil in a frying pan and add the bacon, onion and sugar. Cook over a medium heat for 7–10 minutes (but remove the bacon after 4 minutes and set aside), stirring occasionally until the onion starts to caramelise. Remove the pan from the heat and add seasoning and most of the thyme.

Roll out the pastry on a lightly floured surface to a rectangle measuring about 30 x 15cm (12 x 6in) and then cut the edges to neaten them. Cut the rectangle in half to give two 15cm (6in) squares. Place the pastry squares on a buttered baking sheet and brush water around the edge of each square.

Spoon the caramelised onion onto each pastry square. Place a bacon rasher onto the onion and scatter with the cheese. Bring one side up over the filling, then wrap over the other side, and press together to seal. Brush the pasties with egg glaze and scatter with thyme leaves.

Bake the pasties in the centre of the oven for 20–30 minutes until the pastry has risen and is golden in colour. Serve immediately with crunchy radishes.

Sunflower oil 1 tbsp
Smoked back bacon 2 rashers, de-rinded
Onion 1, peeled and sliced
Caster sugar 1 tsp
Salt and freshly ground black pepper

Chopped thyme 1 tbsp (or 1 tsp dried)
Puff pastry ½ x 500g pack
Gruyère cheese 50g (2oz), grated
Egg 1, beaten for glaze
Radishes to serve, optional

Cook's tip
Instead of using egg for a glaze, the pastries may be brushed with a little milk, although they will then not be as shiny.

Shopper's tip
Buy dry-cured back bacon, so that there isn't a lot of moisture coming out of the bacon as it cooks in the pasties.

Preparation time	10 minutes
Cooking time	40 minutes
Calories per portion	885 Kcal
Fat per portion	59g
of which saturated	21.4g
Serves	2
Suitable for freezing	

...... puff pastry
Sausage meat plait

Pork sausages 4, skinned (approximately 250g/9oz)
Onion 1 small, peeled and finely chopped
Cooking apple 1 peeled, cored and chopped

Chopped sage 1 tbsp (or 1 tsp dried)
Salt and freshly ground black pepper
Puff pastry ½ x 500g pack
Vegetable oil for greasing
Egg 1, beaten for glaze

Preheat the oven to 200°C/400°F/Gas 6. Mix together the sausage meat with the onion, apple, sage and seasoning.

Roll out the pastry on a lightly floured surface to a 30cm (12in) square. Cut around the edges to neaten them. Then make 5–6cm (2–2½in) long cuts on opposite sides of the pastry, at a slight downward angle and about 2.5cm (1in) apart – but not opposite each other, alternate them instead. Brush water around the edges.

Place the sausage meat mixture in the centre of the pastry. Fold down the pastry top, then bring up the cut sides, alternately overlapping them to give a plaited effect, folding up the bottom edge of pastry before bringing over the final side strip. Press the pastry together well at the ends to seal it. Slide the plait onto a lightly greased baking sheet, then brush the pastry with the egg glaze.

Bake the plait in the centre of the oven for 30–40 minutes, or until the pastry has risen and is golden. Remove from the oven and serve either hot or cold.

Cook's tip
Ensure the baking sheet is large enough to take the plait before it's made. If it's not, make the plait shorter, but slightly wider.

Shopper's tip
Look out for all-butter puff pastry for the best flavour, and vary the recipe by using different types of sausages.

Preparation time	10 minutes
Cooking time	45 minutes
Calories per portion	267 Kcal
Fat per portion	12g
of which saturated	1.4g
Serves	2
Suitable for vegetarians + freezing	

…… butternut squash

To make two of the following three recipes, you will need to buy one medium-sized butternut squash. Half the squash is needed for each recipe.

Squash and red pepper soup

Olive oil 1 tbsp
Onion 1 small, peeled and chopped
Butternut squash ½, peeled, deseeded and roughly cubed (400–450g/14–16oz prepared weight)
Red pepper 1 small, deseeded and diced
Thyme a few sprigs
Parsley a few sprigs
Bay leaf 1

Vegetable stock 600ml (1 pint)
Salt and freshly ground black pepper
Lemon juice dash, optional

For the seedy sprinkle
Pumpkin seeds 2 tsp
Sesame seeds 1 tsp
Cumin seeds ½ tsp
Coriander seeds ½ tsp

Put the oil in a large saucepan with the onion, squash, red pepper and herbs. Cover and cook over a medium heat for 10 minutes, stirring occasionally. Then pour the stock into the pan, bring to the boil, lower the heat and let it simmer for 30–35 minutes until the squash is tender.

Meanwhile, mix the seeds in a small pan and heat until they toast and pop. Set them aside in a small dish.

Allow the cooked vegetables to cool for a few minutes, remove the herbs and then purée the mixture either using a stick blender in the pan or transfer to a food processor. Season well and add a dash of lemon juice if you think it tastes too sweet.

Reheat the soup, if necessary, and pour into warmed bowls. Serve with the seeds for sprinkling on top.

Cook's tip
This soup needs no thickening and is also good half puréed – leave a few 'lumps' of squash in it for interest.

Shopper's tip
Butternut squash are available virtually all-year-round and they keep very well for weeks in the vegetable rack.

Preparation time	**10 minutes**
Cooking time	**15 minutes**
Calories per portion	**535 Kcal**
Fat per portion	**26g**
of which saturated	**10.9g**
Serves	**2**
Suitable for vegetarians	

...... butternut squash
Buttery squash with creamy pasta

Olive oil 1 tbsp
Sage leaves 12, 6 left whole, 6 finely chopped
Butternut squash ½, peeled, deseeded and cut into 2cm (¾in) cubes
Red onion 1 small, peeled, cut into wedges and leaves separated
Rigatoni/garganelli or other short pasta 110g (4oz)
Frozen peas 50g (2oz)
Pine nuts 1 tbsp
Salt and freshly ground black pepper
Crème fraîche 4 tbsp
Shaved Parmesan-like cheese 2 tbsp

1. Heat the oil in a medium-sized frying pan, add the whole sage leaves and crisp them for a few seconds then remove from the pan and set aside for the garnish, leaving the flavoured oil in the pan. Add the squash and onion, stir well in the oil, cover and cook for 10 minutes over a medium heat. Shake and stir the pan every so often.

2. Meanwhile, pour boiling water into a large saucepan, add the pasta and cook according to the packet's instructions until just tender. After about 7 minutes add the peas to the pasta pan.

3. Add the pine nuts and chopped sage leaves to the tender squash and stir for a couple of minutes until the nuts turn brown. Season well.

4. When the pasta is cooked, drain it, leaving a little water in the pan. Return the pasta back to the pan and add the crème fraîche and squash mixture and stir gently. Divide between two bowls and garnish with the fried sage leaves and Parmesan cheese.

Cook's tip
Rather than frying the squash and onion, you can roast them for about 40 minutes at 180°C/350°F/Gas 4.

Shopper's tip
Fresh or frozen green beans are fine to use instead of the peas. If you prefer, use white or spring onions instead of the red onion.

Preparation time	10 minutes
Cooking time	55 minutes
Calories per portion	230 Kcal
Fat per portion	12g
of which saturated	4.3g
Serves	2

...... butternut squash
Roast squash with pancetta

Preheat the oven to 190°C/375°F/Gas 5. Cut the squash into 3cm (just over 1in) wedges and place in a shallow, ovenproof dish or roasting tin. Pour the stock over the squash and then sprinkle with the pancetta, thyme sprigs and chilli, if using, and seeds.

Roast in the oven for 45–55 minutes or until the squash is softened and the stock almost absorbed. Remove the thyme sprigs. Serve on its own as a supper dish or as a side dish, perhaps with roast chicken or a pork chop.

Butternut squash ½, peeled, deseeded, and cut into thick slices
Hot vegetable or chicken stock 100ml (3½fl oz)
Pancetta dice 70g pack

Thyme sprigs 4, optional
Red chilli 1 small, deseeded and finely sliced, optional
Pumpkin seeds 1 tbsp
Cumin seeds 1 tsp

Cook's tip
Adding the stock helps stop the squash from sticking to the dish while it cooks. It should not need any oil.

Shopper's tip
If you can't find pancetta dice, use 4 rashers of streaky bacon instead. De-rind and chop them before using.

Cook's tip
Baste the chicken breasts occasionally to prevent them from drying out.

Shopper's tip
For the best flavour, buy skin-on free range or organic chicken breasts for this recipe. You should be able to buy individual vegetables from the green grocer.

Preparation time	**10 minutes**
Cooking time	**1 hour 10 minutes**
Calories per portion	**445 Kcal**
Fat per portion	**14g**
of which saturated	**2.4g**
Serves	**2**

...... chicken

To make two of the following three recipes, you will need to buy one pack of four chicken breasts with their skin on, available in the chiller section of the supermarket. You will need two breasts for each recipe.

Roast chicken dinner for two

Potatoes 2, peeled
Carrot 1, peeled
Parsnip 1, peeled
Olive oil 2 tbsp
Onion 1, peeled and cut into 8 wedges
Garlic 2 cloves, unpeeled
Bay leaves 2
Thyme sprigs 2

Chicken breasts, skin on 2
Salt and freshly ground black pepper
Streaky bacon 2 rashers de-rinded, stretched and halved, optional
Small head of broccoli to serve
Sherry or red wine 2 tbsp, optional
Chicken gravy granules or cornflour 2 tsp

Preheat the oven to 200°C/400°F/Gas 6 and put a large roasting tin in the oven to heat up. Cut the potatoes into 3 or 4 even-sized chunks and put in a medium-sized saucepan with enough water to cover. Cover and bring to the boil.

Cut the carrot and parsnip in half lengthways then half widthways and add to the potatoes after they have been cooking for 5 minutes. Cook for a further 5 minutes. Add 1 tablespoon of the olive oil to the roasting tin to heat up.

Drain the vegetables, reserving the cooking water for cooking the broccoli later. Put the cooked vegetables back in the pan and shake over the heat to dry them and rough up the edges a little.

Add the vegetables to the hot oil in the tin at one end and turn them over to coat in the oil. Add the onion, garlic, bay and thyme at the other end. Use your hand to smooth a little more oil over the chicken breasts and season well. Drizzle the rest of the oil over the vegetables and then roast for 30 minutes.

Place the chicken pieces on top of the thyme, garlic and onion. Turn the vegetables in the tin, roll up the halved rashers of bacon, if using, and add to the tin and roast for 20–30 minutes, until the juices run clear when the centre of the chicken breast is pierced with a knife. Cook the broccoli in the reserved cooking water for about 5 minutes.

When the chicken is cooked, take out of the tin and put on hot plates along with the bacon rolls. Cook the vegetables a bit longer if you like them really crispy. Take them out of the tin and put on the plates.

When the broccoli is cooked, drain but add about 200ml (7fl oz) of the vegetable cooking water to the roasting tin and scrape up all the juices and sticky bits. Pour the juices into a small saucepan, add the sherry or red wine, if using, bring to the boil and thicken with the chicken gravy granules or cornflour. Serve the gravy with the chicken and vegetables.

Preparation time	10 minutes
Marinating time	30 minutes
Cooking time	10 minutes
Calories per portion	303 Kcal
Fat per portion	18g
of which saturated	7.9g
Serves	2
Suitable for freezing	

...... *chicken*

Fragrant chicken escalopes with olive butter

Chicken breasts, skin on 2
Olive oil 1 tbsp
Chopped parsley, tarragon or oregano (or a mixture) 2 tbsp
Lemon ½, grated zest and 2 tbsp juice

Freshly ground black pepper
Butter 25g (1oz)
Green or black olives 4, stoned and finely chopped
Courgette and green beans to serve, optional

Remove sinews and the skin from the chicken breasts. Place them between two sheets of cling film and beat out to about 5mm/¼in thick all over with a meat mallet or rolling pin.

Mix the oil, just over half of the chopped herbs, the lemon zest and juice in a shallow bowl. Add some pepper and then coat the flattened chicken well in the marinade and leave for 30 minutes, or longer if you like, turning them occasionally if you can.

To make the olive butter, soften the butter in a small bowl and add the rest of the chopped herbs and the olives. Put in a small dish and set aside until ready to serve.

Heat a griddle pan to medium high. Put both escalopes on the griddle and press down with a palette knife. Leave for at least 3 minutes to ensure the chicken is sealed before turning over and cooking for another 2–3 minutes. Serve the escalopes whole or cut into two or three pieces on a bed of courgette ribbons and green beans and with the olive butter melting on top.

Cook's tip
Steam the green beans for 5 minutes and add the courgette ribbons (with a pinch of salt) 1 minute before the end.

Shopper's tip
Buy the best-quality olives that you can – with stones in and in olive oil. They will keep in the jar for a few weeks.

Preparation time	5 minutes
Cooking time	27 minutes
Calories per portion	297 Kcal
Fat per portion	4g
of which saturated	0.5g
Serves	2

…… chicken

Lemon chicken soup

Pour the stock into a large saucepan. Bring to the boil and add the carrot, celery and the rice. Reduce the heat to low and leave to simmer for 10 minutes.

Add the chicken and simmer for 15 minutes, then check that the rice and vegetables are just cooked. Remove the chicken, cut off the skin and cut the meat into strips.

Stir the lemon zest and juice into the soup, add the spring onions and half of the parsley and season to taste. Divide the strips of meat between two warmed soup bowls and then spoon the soup over the top. Sprinkle with the rest of the parsley and the almonds, if using.

Home-made or ready made chicken stock 600ml (1 pint)
Carrot 1, peeled and diced
Celery 1 stick, diced
Basmati or long grain rice 2 tbsp
Chicken breasts, skin on 2
Lemon ½, grated zest and 2 tbsp juice

Spring onions 2, trimmed, washed and finely sliced
Chopped parsley 2 tbsp
Salt and freshly ground black pepper
Toasted flaked almonds 1 tbsp, optional

Cook's tip
Good homemade stock makes such a difference to a soup, so it is definitely worth the effort. Stock freezes for up to 3 months.

Shopper's tip
Pots of stock in the fridge or freezer are always useful. Prices of ready-made stock will motivate you to make your own!

Preparation time	**5 minutes**
Cooking time	**15 minutes**
Calories per portion	**829 Kcal**
Fat per portion	**57g**
of which saturated	**26.8g**
Serves	**2**

...... bacon and mushrooms

To make two of the following three recipes, buy one pack of eight rashers of bacon plus a 500g punnet of mushrooms. You will need four of the rashers and half of the mushrooms for each recipe.

Bacon and mushroom tagliatelle

Tagliatelle 150g (5oz)
Sunflower oil 1 tbsp
Smoked back bacon 4
rashers, de-rinded and chopped
Button mushrooms ½ x 500g
punnet, wiped and sliced

Double cream 142ml carton
Pesto sauce 1 tbsp
**Salt and freshly ground
black pepper**
Basil leaves to garnish,
optional

1. Bring a large pan of water to the boil and cook the tagliatelle for 10–12 minutes, or as directed on the pack, until it is just tender.

2. Heat the sunflower oil in a medium-sized saucepan and add the bacon and cook for 2–3 minutes. Then add the mushrooms and cook for a further 4–5 minutes over a medium heat until the mushrooms are very tender. Stir the cream into the pan and simmer the sauce for 1–2 minutes until it thickens slightly, add the pesto sauce and season to taste.

3. Drain the pasta well and add to the pan, and stir it into the sauce. Serve immediately garnished with basil leaves.

Cook's tip
Crème fraîche is a tasty alternative to the double cream and it works just as well.

Shopper's tip
Choose dry tagliatelle rather than fresh, because the rest of the pack will then keep for a long time in an airtight container.

Preparation time	5 minutes
Cooking time	30 minutes
Calories per portion	479 Kcal
Fat per portion	20g
of which saturated	6.4g
Serves	2

...... bacon and mushrooms

Bacon and mushroom risotto

Heat the sunflower oil in a medium-sized saucepan and add the onion. Cook the onion for 3–5 minutes until it starts to soften, then add the bacon and mushrooms and cook for a further 7–10 minutes over a medium heat, until the bacon is cooked and the mushrooms have softened.

Add the rice to the pan and cook for about 1 minute, stirring continually. Add the wine and simmer gently until most of the liquid has dissolved, stirring regularly so that it does not stick to the base of the pan.

Dissolve the stock cube in 300ml (½ pint) of boiling water and add to the pan. Stir until the stock cube dissolves. Simmer the rice gently, stirring it occasionally for 12–15 minutes, or until all the water is absorbed. If the mixture thickens and the rice is not tender, then add some extra boiling water, but take care not to overcook the rice.

When the rice is tender, season to taste and serve the risotto with basil leaves and Parmesan cheese sprinkled on top.

Sunflower oil 1 tbsp
Onion 1, peeled and chopped
Smoked back bacon 4 rashers, de-rinded and chopped
Button mushrooms ½ x 500g punnet, wiped and sliced
Risotto rice 110–150g (4–5oz)
White wine 125ml (4fl oz)
Boiling water 300–450ml (½–¾ pint)
Ham or vegetable stock cube 1
Salt and freshly ground black pepper
Grated or shaved Parmesan cheese for sprinkling
Basil leaves to garnish

Cook's tip
To make the recipe more colourful, stir in a few halved cherry tomatoes towards the end of the cooking time.

Shopper's tip
Look out for the small size bottles of wine and use half here. The rest may be kept in the fridge for up to a week.

107

Cook's tip

If you like garlic, then you can rub the bread with a cut clove before brushing the olive oil over it to give a garlic bread base.

Shopper's tip

If possible, to give a chunky croûte, choose a rustic bread and cut it with a knife rather than buying it pristinely ready-sliced.

Preparation time	5 minutes
Cooking time	10 minutes
Calories per portion	402 Kcal
Fat per portion	23g
of which saturated	7.1g
Serves	2

...... bacon and mushrooms
Bacon and mushroom croutes

Olive oil 3 tbsp
White or wholemeal bread 2 thick slices
Smoked back bacon 4 rashers, de-rinded
Button mushrooms ½ x 500g punnet,
wiped and sliced

Eggs 3, lightly beaten
Snipped chives 2 tbsp
Salt and freshly ground black pepper

Preheat the grill to hot. Lightly brush both sides of the slices of bread with some of the olive oil, place them under the grill and toast until lightly golden. Then turn over the slices and toast the other side.

Meanwhile, heat the remaining oil in a frying pan, add the bacon and mushrooms, and cook over a medium heat for 5–7 minutes, or until softened.

Add the eggs and 2 tablespoons of water to the pan and stir gently as the egg is setting to give lightly scrambled egg. Stir the chives into the pan and season with salt and pepper.

Place the bread on two serving plates, top with the bacon and mushroom mixture and serve immediately.

Preparation time	**10 minutes**
Cooking time	**20 minutes**
Calories per portion	**825 Kcal**
Fat per portion	**54g**
of which saturated	**26.1g**
Serves	**2**
Suitable for freezing	

...... ham

To make two of the following three recipes, you will need to buy a 250g pack (or from the deli counter) of quality cooked ham. You will need 125g (4½oz) for each recipe.

Ham and green pea soup

Olive oil 1 tbsp
Onion 1, peeled and chopped
Garlic 1 clove, peeled and finely chopped
Frozen peas 450g (1lb)
Cooked ham 125g (4½oz), chopped

Chicken or vegetable stock 450ml (¾ pint)
Salt and freshly ground black pepper
Double cream 142ml pot
Toasted croutons 60g pack

Heat the olive oil in a large saucepan and cook the onion and garlic until softened. Add the peas and 75g (3oz) of the ham and mix well. Add the stock, bring slowly to the boil, then reduce the heat and simmer for 15 minutes, skimming off any scum that forms.

Pour into a food processor and blend until smooth. Return to the pan, heat gently and season with salt and pepper.

Serve the hot soup in individual bowls garnished with a swirl of cream, the remaining chopped ham and croutons.

Cook's tip
Making a ham sandwich? Use up the leftover ham by making this brilliant and filling soup! It's a meal in one.

Shopper's tip
Look out for packets of fresh croutons to serve with this soup. They are found in the salad section of the supermarket.

Preparation time	5 minutes
Cooking time	12 minutes
Calories per portion	654 Kcal
Fat per portion	30g
of which saturated	13.5g
Serves	2

...... ham

Ham carbonara

Spaghetti 175g (6oz)
Olive oil 1 tbsp
Garlic 1 clove, peeled and finely chopped
Cooked ham 125g (4½oz), cut into strips

Single cream 142ml pot
Egg 1
Parmesan cheese 25g (1oz), grated
Freshly ground black pepper

1 Cook the spaghetti in a pan of boiling water according to the packet's instructions.

2 Meanwhile, heat the oil in a large frying pan and cook the garlic and ham for 5 minutes, stirring occasionally. Mix together the single cream with the egg and most of the Parmesan cheese.

3 Drain the pasta and quickly tip back into the pan. Stir the cream mixture and ham into the pasta and quickly mix well so that the egg doesn't curdle. Serve at once in two warmed pasta bowls. Garnish with pepper and the remaining Parmesan cheese.

Cook's tip
For a really speedy dish, buy fresh spaghetti, which cooks quickly. Dinner will be ready in just 5 minutes!

Shopper's tip
Visit your local deli and ask them to recommend a good cured ham. Use this instead of the ordinary ham.

Preparation time	5 minutes
Cooking time	7 minutes
Calories per omelette	492 Kcal
Fat per omelette	37g
of which saturated	15.8g
Makes	2 omelettes

...... ham
Cheese and ham soufflé omelette

Beat the egg yolks with the tarragon, if using. Whisk the egg whites to a peak, then fold into the yolk mixture with the seasoning, half of the cheese and all of the ham.

Preheat the grill to hot. On the hob, heat 1 teaspoon of the olive oil in a small omelette pan (with a heatproof handle), pour half of the egg mixture into the pan and cook for 1–2 minutes until just beginning to turn golden underneath.

Pop the pan under the preheated grill and, when the mix begins to rise, sprinkle over half of the remaining cheese and return to the grill until the cheese melts – about another 1–2 minutes. Fold the omelette in half as you turn it out onto a warm plate and serve with a little extra pepper. Repeat steps 2 and 3 for the second omelette.

Eggs 4, separated
Finely chopped tarragon 2 tbsp, optional
Salt and freshly ground black pepper

Cheddar cheese 110g (4oz), finely chopped
Cooked ham 125g (4½oz), chopped
Olive oil 2 tsp

Cook's tip
If you are cooking for one, simply halve all of the ingredients and follow the method as usual. It makes a deliciously easy meal.

Shopper's tip
For a special treat, substitute the smoked salmon for the ham and enjoy the omelette with a glass of chilled fizz.

Cook's tip

For freezing, make and freeze the beef mixture only. To cook, allow to thaw for 2 hours, then prepare the potatoes as below, arrange them on top of the beef, brush with butter and bake as in step 4.

Shopper's tip

For the best results, use good-quality minced beef or buy lean braising steak and mince it yourself.

Preparation time	30 minutes
Cooking time	50–60 minutes
Calories per portion	690 Kcal
Fat per portion	29g
of which saturated	12.6g
Serves	2
Suitable for freezing	

...... minced beef

To make two of the following three recipes, you will need to buy a 500g pack of lean minced beef. You will need 250g (9oz) for each recipe.

Chilli beef pie

Potatoes 610g (1¼lb), peeled and thinly sliced
Sunflower oil 1 tbsp
Onion 1 large, peeled and finely chopped
Ground chilli powder ½ tsp
Lean minced beef 250g (9oz)

Beef stock cube ½
Kidney beans 150g (5oz) (drained weight), rinsed
Chopped tomatoes 227g can
Butter 25g (1oz), melted

Preheat the oven to 220°C/425°F/Gas 7. Put the sliced potatoes into a saucepan, cover with cold water and bring to the boil, then drain well.

Meanwhile, heat the oil in a large frying pan, add the onion and cook gently until softened but not browned. Stir in the chilli powder, add the beef and continue cooking just until the meat changes colour. Remove the frying pan from the heat, add the stock cube and stir until it dissolves in the pan juices.

Mix the kidney beans and chopped tomatoes into the meat and then transfer into a shallow, 1.25 litre (2 pint) baking dish. Arrange the sliced potatoes, slightly overlapping, on top of the meat and then brush well with the melted butter.

Place the pie on a baking sheet and cook in the centre of the oven for 50–60 minutes, or until the potato topping is cooked and golden brown.

Preparation time	10 minutes
Chilling time	1 hour
Cooking time	15 minutes
Calories per portion	692 Kcal
Fat per portion	37g
of which saturated	12.2g
Serves	2
Suitable for freezing	

...... minced beef
Peppered meatballs

Stuffing mix 90g (3½oz)
Boiling water 125ml (4fl oz)
Olive oil 2 tbsp
Onion 1 small, peeled and finely chopped
Egg 1 large, beaten
Lean minced beef 250g (9oz)
Coarsely ground black

peppercorns 1 tsp
White wine 300ml (½ pint)
Double cream 2 tbsp
Buttered tagliatelle to serve, optional
Chopped basil or parsley to garnish, optional

1. Put the stuffing in a bowl, add the boiling water, stir and leave to stand. Heat 1 tablespoon of the oil in a small frying pan, add the onion and cook until softened. Remove from the heat and allow the onion to cool.

2. Add the cooled onion, beaten egg and the minced beef to the stuffing and mix. Divide into 8–10 pieces and roll each one between your hands into a smooth ball. Roll in the crushed peppercorns (on a plate). Cover the meatballs and chill for an hour to firm up the mixture and make them easier to cook.

3. When ready to cook, heat the remaining oil in a frying pan, add the meatballs and cook for 4–5 minutes, turning frequently until they are lightly browned and cooked through. Transfer onto a plate, cover and keep warm.

4. Skim off any excess fat from the frying pan, then add the wine and bring to the boil, stirring and scraping any residue from the bottom of the pan. Reduce the heat to low and allow the pan juices to bubble gently until reduced by about a third. Then stir the cream into the wine and heat through gently – taking care not to let the sauce boil.

5. To serve, place the meatballs on a bed of buttered tagliatelle and strain the sauce over the top. Garnish with herbs, if using.

Cook's tip
Crush whole peppercorns in a mortar with a pestle or with a rolling pin between two sheets of greaseproof paper.

Shopper's tip
For the best taste, choose Country stuffing mix if you can. If this is not available, experiment with other flavours.

Preparation time	20 minutes
Chilling time	30–40 minutes
Cooking time	6–8 minutes
Calories per burger	486 Kcal
Fat per burger	32g
of which saturated	10.9g
Serves	2
Suitable for freezing	

...... minced beef
Swedish-style burgers

Put the onion, sausage meat, beef, capers and beetroot into a large mixing bowl and mix together, adding just 1–2 tablespoons of the beaten egg to bind – don't add too much as the mixture will be too wet.

Divide the mixture into two and shape by hand into two large burgers, about 1cm (½in) thick. If possible, chill the burgers for 30–40 minutes before cooking.

Heat the sunflower oil in a frying pan, add the burgers and cook for 3–4 minutes on each side – take care not to overcook, as they will become dry. Serve each burger on a toasted bun with some sliced gerkins, relish and salad leaves.

Onion 1 small, peeled and very finely chopped
Pork sausages 2 (approximately 150g/5oz), skinned
Lean minced beef 250g (9oz)
Capers 1–2 tsp, drained

Pickled beetroot 50g (2oz), cut into small dice
Egg 1, beaten
Sunflower oil 1–2 tbsp
Toasted buns to serve
Gerkins, relish and salad to serve, optional

Cook's tip
To freeze the burgers, make up to the end of step 2. Wrap individually in cling film and foil. Thaw and cook as in step 3.

Shopper's tip
For the best results, buy the best quality minced beef you can find or buy lean braising steak and mince it yourself.

Special occasions

There are some real treats in store in this chapter. Specifically written for an occasion when you want to push the boat out a little – special food is not just for large dinner parties – these meals are truly delicious.

Who needs to book a restaurant table when you can have venison with cranberries or honey roast salmon? Enjoy the pleasure of cooking and the pleasure of good company accompanied by truly divine food.

Choose your favourite companion and treat them to a meal to remember. After all, with meals this good you'll be tempted to celebrate Valentine's Day every day of the year!

Preparation time	10 minutes
Cooking time	15 minutes
Calories per portion	596 Kcal
Fat per portion	45g
of which saturated	10g
Serves	2

Salmon with minty papaya and avocado salsa

Salmon fillets 2 (approximately 150g (5oz) each), skinned
Lime ½, grated zest and juice
Butter 15g (½oz)
Salt and freshly ground black pepper

Cooked rice to serve, optional

For the salsa
Olive oil 2 tbsp
Lime ½, grated zest and juice
Papaya ½–1 small, peeled, deseeded and chopped
Avocado 1, stoned, peeled and chopped
Chopped mint 2 tbsp

Preheat the oven to 200°C/400°F/Gas 6. To prepare the salmon, brush the lime juice over the fish. Place a knob of butter on each fillet and scatter with the lime zest and season with salt and pepper.

Place the fish on a buttered baking sheet and bake in the centre of the oven for 12–15 minutes, or until it is just starting to turn golden in colour.

To make the salsa, tip the olive oil, lime zest and juice into a bowl and add the papaya, avocado and mint. Mix well. Season to taste.

Serve the fish on a bed of rice. with the salsa spooned on to the plate.

Cook's tip
If the papaya is large, then only use half of it. Keep the other half wrapped in a plastic bag in the fridge for up to 2 days.

Shopper's tip
Make sure the avocado and papaya are ripe to get the best flavours. Buy the fruits a few days early and allow them to ripen.

Preparation time	**5 minutes**
Cooking time	**12–15 minutes**
Calories per portion	**310 Kcal**
Fat per portion	**18g**
of which saturated	**3.3g**
Serves	**2**

Honey roast mustard salmon

Salmon steaks 2 (approximately 300g/11oz)
Salt and freshly ground black pepper
Wholegrain mustard 2 tsp
Balsamic vinegar 2 tsp
Clear honey 2 tsp
Steamed baby vegetables to serve, optional
Roast new potatoes to serve, optional

1 Preheat the oven to 200°C/400°F/ Gas 6. Wash and pat dry the salmon and add seasoning. Place on a small baking tray lined with greaseproof paper.

2 Mix together the remaining ingredients and spread thickly over the salmon. Bake for 12–15 minutes, depending on thickness, until the steaks are cooked through. Serve the salmon on a bed of diagonally sliced and steamed baby vegetables with roast new potatoes.

Cook's tip
Why not roast some diced baby potatoes with olive oil for 10 minutes before putting the salmon in the oven – they will be ready at the same time.

Shopper's tip
Choose salmon with the skin on for easier baking.

Preparation time	10 minutes
Cooking time	10 minutes
Calories per portion	837 Kcal
Fat per portion	47g
of which saturated	30.0g
Serves	2

Thai green curry with lime rice

Heat the sunflower oil in a medium-sized saucepan and add the chicken. Cook over a medium heat, stirring occasionally for 5–7 minutes, until the chicken has started to turn golden. Add the Thai curry paste and cook for a further 1–2 minutes, stirring continually.

Pour the coconut milk into the pan and bring to the boil, then reduce the heat and simmer for 10 minutes, to cook the chicken. Add the vegetables and cook for 3–4 minutes, or until the vegetables are just tender. Add fish sauce to taste, if using.

Cut the top off the pack of microwave rice and add the lime zest and juice to the pack. Cook the rice in a microwave according to the pack instructions and then stir it well to mix with the lime.

Spoon the rice into bowls, pour the curry over the top and serve immediately.

Sunflower oil 1 tbsp
Skinless chicken breasts 2 (approximately 200g (7oz) each), chopped
Thai green curry paste 3 tbsp
Coconut milk 400g can

Stir-fry vegetables 300g pack
Fish sauce dash, optional
Microwave jasmine or basmati rice 250g pack
Lime 1, grated zest and juice

Cook's tip
Microwave rice is very quick and easy; alternatively, you could boil some jasmine rice and stir in the lime zest and juice at the end.

Shopper's tip
This recipe can be varied by using different combinations of stir-fry vegetables – any type will work well.

Keep a tub of breadcrumbs in the freezer. Freeze them on a baking sheet before transferring to the tub and you can then use them by the handful from frozen.

Shopper's tip
Vary the herbs you buy so they are different from those you have in the garden or on your windowsill. Oregano, tarragon, basil or chives would be fine in the mixture.

Preparation time	10 minutes
Cooking time	35–40 minutes
Calories per portion	598 Kcal
Fat per portion	35g
of which saturated	12.3g
Serves	2

Springtime rack of lamb

New potatoes 8–10 small, scrubbed
Chantenay or baby carrots 150g (5oz), scrubbed
Olive oil 2 tbsp
Extra lean rack of lamb 250g (9oz)
English or wholegrain mustard 1 tbsp

Small shallots 3, left unpeeled
White breadcrumbs 6 tbsp
Chopped parsley 1 tbsp
Chopped rosemary 1 tbsp
Salt and freshly ground black pepper

1   Preheat the oven to 200°C/400°F/Gas 6. Put a roasting tin in the oven to heat up. Add the potatoes to a pan of boiling water, bring back to the boil and add the carrots. Simmer for 5 minutes then drain well.

2   Heat a frying pan, rub a little of the oil over the lamb rack and seal it in the pan for about 1 minute on each side. Remove from the pan and spread the mustard on the fleshy side of the lamb.

3   Peel and finely chop one of the shallots and mix with the breadcrumbs, herbs and seasoning and 2 teaspoons of the oil. Mix and bind together with your hands, then press it onto the lamb.

4   Put the coated lamb, the remaining 2 unpeeled shallots and the parboiled potatoes and carrots in the roasting tin and drizzle with the rest of the oil. Roast for 20 minutes (the lamb will still be pink in the middle, so cook for 5–10 minutes longer if you prefer it well done).

5   Take the lamb out of the oven and leave it to rest, loosely covered in foil, for 10 minutes. Continue to cook the potatoes and carrots for another 10 minutes until browned. Cut through the lamb bone with a big knife, cutting it into two pieces, or cut down between each chop. Serve with the roasted vegetables.

Preparation time	10 minutes
Cooking time	2½ hours
Calories per portion	790 Kcal
Fat per portion	43g
of which saturated	18.6g
Serves	2
Suitable for freezing	

Braised lamb shanks

Olive oil 1 tbsp
Lamb shanks 2 (approximately 450g (1lb) each)
Onion 1, peeled and sliced
Carrot 1, peeled and sliced
Garlic 1 clove, peeled and chopped
Rosemary 1 sprig
Bay leaf 1
Sherry 2 tbsp
Chopped tomatoes 400g can
Lamb stock cube 1

Salt and freshly ground black pepper
Puy lentils 50g (2oz)
Cornflour 2 tsp
Redcurrant jelly 2 tsp, optional
Fish sauce or soy sauce a good dash, optional
Sweet potato mash to serve, optional
Parsley sprigs to garnish, optional

1. Preheat the oven to 160°C/325°F/Gas 3. Heat the oil in a flameproof casserole and brown the lamb shanks all over, for 6–8 minutes. Remove from the casserole and set aside.

2. Add the onion, carrot and garlic to the pan, cover and cook over a medium heat for 5 minutes to soften them. Add the rosemary, bay leaf and sherry, then stir in the can of tomatoes, the crumbled stock cube and a can full of hot water (400ml/14fl oz). Return the shanks, bring to the boil, season, put on the lid and cook in the oven for 1 hour.

3. After an hour, turn the lamb shanks and add the lentils. Cook for another hour and then take the lid off the casserole and thicken the sauce, if you like, by blending the cornflour with 3 teaspoons of water and stirring it into the sauce. Add the redcurrant jelly, if using, to make the sauce glossy. Return to the oven for 30 minutes.

4. Just before serving, taste the sauce and add a good dash of fish or soy sauce, if using. Serve each shank on a bed of sweet potato mash, garnished with parsley.

Cook's tip
Store leftover sauce in the fridge, then thin down with hot water and serve as soup for two people another day.

Shopper's tip
Buy lamb shanks from a butcher or supermarket when you see them, especially if cn offer – they freeze well.

Preparation time	10 minutes
Cooking time	20 minutes
Calories per portion	481 Kcal
Fat per portion	20g
of which saturated	2.6g
Serves	2

Venison with cranberry on garlic mash

Potatoes 3–4, peeled and cut into chunks
Garlic 1–2 cloves, peeled
Venison steaks 2 (approximately 150g/5oz each)
Salt and freshly ground black pepper
Sunflower oil 1 tbsp
Cranberry sauce 4 tbsp
Beef stock cube 1
Chopped rosemary 1 tbsp
Olive oil 2 tbsp

Place the potatoes and garlic cloves in a medium-sized saucepan and cover with water. Bring to the boil, lower the heat and simmer for 15–20 minutes, or until the potatoes are tender.

Meanwhile, season both sides of the venison steaks with salt and pepper. Heat the sunflower oil in a frying pan and add the venison. Cook for 2–3 minutes on each side until the venison has started to brown. Remove the steaks from the pan.

Add the cranberry sauce, 150ml (¼ pint) water and the stock cube to the pan, and stir until the cranberry sauce melts and the stock cube dissolves. Then simmer gently until the sauce thickens slightly. Add the rosemary to the sauce, then return the venison to the pan and simmer gently for 3–5 minutes, or until the venison is cooked to your liking.

Drain the potatoes and garlic, return them to their saucepan and add the olive oil. Season to taste and then mash the potatoes. Slice the venison and serve on a bed of the mash with the sauce spooned over the top.

Cook's tip
Take care not to overcook the venison or it will become tough.

Shopper's tip
If you don't want to have to buy a whole bulb of garlic, then omit the garlic and use garlic salt as the seasoning in the potato when it's mashed.

Preparation time	20 minutes
Cooking time	35–40 minutes
Calories per portion	646 Kcal
Fat per portion	31g
of which saturated	16.9g
Serves	2

Tournedos of beef with asparagus

Large baking potato(es)
450g (1lb) (1–2, depending on size), peeled and thinly sliced
Butter 50g (2oz), melted
Salt
Fillet steak 2 (150–175g (5–6oz) each)

Mixed peppercorns 1 tsp, crushed
Asparagus spears 6–8, woody ends snapped or cut off
Red wine 150ml (¼ pint)
Beef stock 150ml (¼ pint)
Caster sugar 1 tsp

1 Preheat the oven to 220°C/425°F/Gas 7. Line a baking tray with non-stick foil. Using a saucer, mark out two circles on the foil.

2 Place one slice of potato in the centre of each circle, and then arrange a ring of overlapping potatoes on top. Brush with a little of the melted butter and season. Repeat and then bake for 45–50 minutes, until the potatoes are golden brown.

3 Meanwhile, season the steaks with salt and the crushed peppercorns. Gently cook the asparagus in a wide, shallow frying pan for 4–5 minutes, or until just tender. Drain and keep warm.

4 When the potato galettes are almost cooked, heat the remaining butter in a frying pan until sizzling. Add the steaks and cook for 3–4 minutes on each side. Remove from the pan and keep warm.

5 Skim off excess fat from the frying pan. Add the wine, stock and sugar and bring to the boil, stirring and scraping the browned residue from the bottom. Allow the sauce to bubble gently until reduced by about half. Transfer the potato galettes onto warmed plates and place the steaks and asparagus on top. Serve with the gravy.

Cook's tip
This recipe isn't as difficult to make as it may seem – the secret is to be well organised.

Shopper's tip
For the very best flavour, buy the steak from a reputable, traditional butcher.

Preparation time	5 minutes
Cooking time	10 minutes
Calories per portion	485 Kcal
Fat per portion	22g
of which saturated	8g
Serves	2

Beef stroganoff with rice

1. Bring a saucepan of water to the boil and add the rice. Cover, reduce the heat and simmer for 10 minutes, or as indicated on the packet.

2. Meanwhile, heat the oil in a large frying pan until very hot, add the meat and stir-fry for a couple of minutes over a high heat until the meat is browned.

3. Remove the meat from the pan and add the shallots and garlic and cook until softened. Add the mushrooms and cook for a further minute or two. Return the meat to the pan.

4. Add the brandy to the beef gravy and pour into the meat mixture. Cook for 2–3 minutes or until hot and the meat is tender.

5. When the rice is cooked, drain and rinse with hot water. Divide the rice between two plates, add a portion of stroganoff, season with black pepper and garnish with paprika. Serve immediately with green beans.

Basmati rice 250g (9oz)
Prime fillet beef steak 350g (12oz), cut into strips
Olive oil 1 tbsp
Shallots 2, peeled and thinly sliced
Garlic 1 clove, peeled and finely chopped

Baby button mushrooms 100g pack, wiped and halved
Brandy 1 tbsp, optional
Beef gravy 200ml (7fl oz)
Paprika and black pepper to garnish
Green beans to serve, optional

Cook's tip
For a really decadent dish, serve the stroganoff with some delicious soured cream.

Shopper's tip
Buy ready-made fresh beef gravy. It comes in 500g pots and this recipe uses just under half that quantity.

Freeze easy

How did people manage before freezers? They keep food fresh and nutritious for months, and are invaluable in the small household.

Did you cook too much, or take up a last-minute invitation to eat out? No problem: pop your creation in the freezer and enjoy it another time. All these recipes serve four, so they are great for feeding one person on four occasions – or two people on two occasions.

The freezer isn't just for chips and ice cream: look out for the mushroom and Stilton cannelloni or beef casserole, followed by pear and cinnamon crumble. Cook just once and enjoy the fruits of your labour on several occasions.

Preparation time	20 minutes
Cooking time	1 hour 5 minutes
Calories per portion	532 Kcal
Fat per portion	18g
of which saturated	3.8g
Serves	4

Suitable for vegetarians + freezing

Root vegetable casserole with cornbread topping

For the vegetable casserole

Vegetable oil 1 tbsp
Onion 1, peeled and chopped
Garlic 1 clove, peeled and chopped
Celery 2 sticks, trimmed and chopped
Carrot 1 large, peeled and chopped
Potato 1 large, peeled and chopped
Parsnip 1, peeled and chopped
Sweet potato 1 small, peeled and chopped
Vegetable stock 300ml (½ pint)
Chopped tomatoes with garlic 400g can

Dried thyme 1 tsp
Salt and freshly ground black pepper

For the cornbread topping

Fine cornmeal 225g (8oz)
Plain flour 2 tbsp
Baking powder 4 tsp
Eggs 3, beaten
Whole milk 175ml (6fl oz)
Vegetable oil 2 tbsp

First prepare the vegetable casserole. Heat the oil in a large saucepan and gently fry the onion, garlic and celery for 5 minutes until just softened but not browned. Add the other vegetables along with the stock and tomatoes. Bring to the boil and add the thyme and seasoning. Cover and simmer for about 30 minutes until tender.

Preheat the oven to 220°C/425°F/Gas 7. Transfer the vegetables to a shallow ovenproof dish and set aside while preparing the topping. Mix the cornmeal, flour and baking powder in a bowl. Make a well in the centre and bind together with the eggs, milk and oil.

Spoon the batter over the vegetables and bake in the oven for 25–30 minutes until golden and firm. Serve immediately or cool and freeze as described opposite.

Preparation time	15 minutes
Cooking time	1¼ hours
Calories per portion	390 Kcal
Fat per portion	21g
of which saturated	9.4g
Serves	4

Suitable for vegetarians + freezing

Mushroom and Stilton cannelloni in a tomato sauce

For the filling
Boiling water 150ml (¼ pint)
Dried mushrooms 15g (½oz)
Olive oil 1 tbsp
Onion 1, peeled and chopped
Chestnut mushrooms 250g (9oz), wiped and finely chopped
White breadcrumbs 25g (1oz)
Stilton 150g (5oz), crumbled
Chopped parsley 4 tbsp
Salt and freshly ground black pepper

For the sauce
Chopped tomatoes 400g can
Sugar good pinch

Lasagne 8 sheets
Pine nuts 2 tbsp
Green salad to serve, optional

To make the filling, pour the boiling water over the dried mushrooms and leave them to soak for 10 minutes. Heat the oil in a frying pan and cook the onion over a medium heat for about 8 minutes. Add the fresh mushrooms and cook for 4 minutes. Then drain the rehydrated mushrooms, reserving the liquid. Chop them if large and add to the pan and cook for another 3 minutes.

Spoon the mixture into a bowl and leave to cool for 5 minutes before adding the breadcrumbs, most of the Stilton and the parsley. Season to taste.

To make the sauce, mix the strained liquid from the mushrooms with 100ml (3½fl oz) water, the tomatoes and sugar. Bring to the boil and simmer for 8–10 minutes.

Precook the lasagne in boiling salted water, then transfer to a large bowl of cold water.

Preheat the oven to 200°C/400°F/Gas 6 and lightly butter two shallow ovenproof dishes. Pour about a quarter of the tomato sauce into each dish. Lay the lasagne sheets on the work surface. Divide the stuffing mixture between the lasagne sheets, then roll them up and pack into the two dishes. Spoon the rest of the sauce over the top and sprinkle with the pine nuts and reserved Stilton.

Cover the dish with oiled foil and cook for 30 minutes. Then remove the foil and cook for 10 minutes to brown the nuts. Serve with salad.

Cook's tip
Freeze uncooked for cooking in the oven later. Cover with cling film, seal well, label and freeze. Thaw in the fridge for 6 hours.

Shopper's tip
Dried mushrooms may seem pricey, but they do accentuate the flavour of fresh mushrooms and keep well in a jam jar or tub.

Preparation time	15 minutes
Cooking time	45 minutes
Calories per tartlet	425 Kcal
Fat per tartlet	29g
of which saturated	11.4g
Serves	4
Suitable for freezing	

Salmon and green bean tartlets

Shortcrust pastry 200g (7oz)
Green beans 110g (4oz), trimmed and cut roughly into 2.5cm (1in) lengths
Fresh salmon fillet 225g (8oz)

Chopped parsley 2 tbsp
Egg 1 large
Single cream 142ml pot
Salt and freshly ground black pepper

Lightly grease four 10cm (4in) diameter, loose-based tartlet tins. Roll out the pastry to a strip about 40 x 22.5cm (16 x 9in) and cut out three rounds big enough to line three of the tins. Press the pastry in gently and leave it about 5mm (¼in) higher than the top of the tins. Re-roll the trimmings and use to line the fourth tin. Prick the bases and sides well, then put the cases in the freezer for 15 minutes while the oven heats up and you make the filling. Preheat the oven to 190°C/375°F/Gas 5. Put a baking sheet in the oven to heat up.

Add the beans to a saucepan of boiling water and cook for 3 minutes. Remove the beans and add the salmon to the water in the pan, cover and gently poach the fish for 3 minutes. Remove and leave to cool for 10 minutes.

Line the frozen tartlets with foil, and bake on the hot baking sheet for 10 minutes. Remove the foil and bake for another 5 minutes or until the pastry is browned. Take them out of the oven. Turn down the oven temperature to 160°C/325°F/Gas 3.

Skin the fish, break it into large flakes and divide it between the cases with the parsley and beans. Whisk the egg and cream in a jug, season well and pour over the filling. Bake for 20–25 minutes until just set. Leave for 5 minutes, then remove from the tins. Serve warm or cold.

Cook's tip
Freeze when cool. Wrap in foil, seal and label. Use within 2 months. Thaw in the fridge for 4 hours and warm through.

Shopper's tip
Ready-made or home-made shortcrust pastry freezes well, so it's handy to have in the freezer.

Preparation time	10 minutes
Cooking time	15 minutes
Calories per burger	211 Kcal
Fat per burger	7g
of which saturated	2.2g
Serves	4
Suitable for freezing	

Chicken and apricot burgers with relish

Chicken or turkey mince 500g (1lb)
Spring onions 4, trimmed and finely sliced
Dried apricots 8, finely chopped
Salt and freshly ground black pepper
Olive oil 1 tbsp
Pitta bread to serve, optional

For the relish (for 2 people)
Greek natural yogurt 4 tbsp
Cucumber 2.5cm (1in) piece, finely chopped
Chopped mint 1 tbsp

Mix the minced chicken or turkey with the spring onions, dried apricots and a generous amount of seasoning. Divide the mixture into four and shape each portion into a burger about 10cm (4in) wide.

Heat a frying pan, add the oil and then two burgers. Leave them to cook over a medium heat for 5 minutes, pressing them down gently with a fish slice. Then turn them over and cook for another 5–6 minutes on the other side.

Meanwhile, make the relish by mixing together all the ingredients. Serve the burgers with the relish and warmed pitta bread.

Cook's tip
To freeze, wrap the raw burgers individually in cling film and pack in a plastic box. Use within 2 months. Thaw in the fridge overnight and cook as above.

Shopper's tip
Buy mince when it's on special offer or mince your own at home.

Preparation time	10 minutes
Cooking time	40 minutes
Calories per portion	437 Kcal
Fat per portion	20g
of which saturated	6g
Serves	4
Suitable for freezing	

Smoky chicken hotpot

Heat a flameproof casserole dish, add the bacon and dry-fry for a few minutes, then add the oil and when hot, add the chicken and chorizo. Cook, stirring occasionally, until the chicken is sealed and the pimiento oil is drawn from the chorizo.

Add the onion and red pepper, put the lid on the pan and cook over a medium heat for 5 minutes.

Add the tomatoes, stock, sugar, chickpeas and half of the parsley. Cover and simmer for 10 minutes, then take the lid off and simmer for another 15–20 minutes to let the sauce thicken. Season to taste.

Serve, sprinkled with the rest of the parsley.

Streaky bacon 4 rashers, de-rinded and each cut into 3 pieces
Olive oil 1 tbsp
Skinless chicken breasts 2 (approximately 200g (7oz) each), chopped
Chorizo sausage 110g (4oz) (pack of 2 cooked sausages), sliced into thick rings
Onion 1, peeled and sliced

Red pepper 1, deseeded and cut into strips
Chopped tomatoes 400g can
Hot chicken stock 300ml (½ pint)
Soft dark brown sugar 1 tbsp
Chickpeas 410g can, rinsed and drained
Chopped parsley 4 tbsp
Salt and freshly ground black pepper

Cook's tip
Freeze when cool and pack in a polybag. Use within 2 months. Thaw in the fridge overnight. Reheat in a pan on the hob.

Shopper's tip
If you are short on time, chicken can also be bought in packs of ready chopped chunks.

Cook's tip

To freeze, allow the meatballs and gravy to cool. Spoon the gravy into a freezer-proof container and add the meatballs. Cover and freeze for up to 6 months. Defrost overnight in the fridge. Reheat in a frying pan until piping hot.

Shopper's tip

Try replacing the turkey with pork for a more traditional combination.

Preparation time	**10 minutes**
Chilling time	**30 minutes**
Cooking time	**42 minutes**
Calories per portion	**353 Kcal**
Fat per portion	**10g**
of which saturated	**1.2g**
Serves	**4**
Suitable for freezing	

Turkey, apple and sage meatballs in onion gravy

Turkey mince 450g (1lb)
Sage and onion stuffing mix 8 tbsp
Apple sauce 4 tbsp
Freshly ground black pepper
Vegetable oil 2 tbsp

Onion 1 large, peeled and thinly sliced
Chicken stock 600ml (1 pint)
Plain flour 1 tbsp
Cooked rice and peas to serve, optional

Put the turkey mince in a bowl, add the stuffing mix and apple sauce and stir well. Season with pepper and bring together to form a firm mixture. Divide into 12 portions and form each into a ball. Place on a plate lined with greaseproof paper, cover and chill for 30 minutes.

Meanwhile, heat 1 tablespoon of the oil in a frying pan and gently fry the onion for about 10 minutes, stirring occasionally, until softened and lightly brown. Drain and set aside to cool.

In the same frying pan, heat the remaining oil and gently fry the turkey meatballs, turning them frequently, for about 5 minutes until sealed all over. Pour in sufficient stock to just cover the bottom of the pan. Bring to the boil, cover, reduce the heat and simmer gently for about 20 minutes to steam the meatballs, until cooked through. Drain, reserving any stock, and set aside – keep warm if planning to serve straightaway.

In the same frying pan, reheat the onions and add the flour. Gradually blend the stock into the flour and bring to the boil, stirring, until thickened. Simmer for 2 minutes. If serving immediately, pour the gravy over the meatballs and serve with rice and peas. Otherwise, allow to cool and freeze as described in the Cook's tip opposite.

Cook's tip
To freeze, allow to cool. Transfer to individual freezer containers. Freeze for up to 6 months. Allow to defrost overnight in the fridge. Reheat in the oven in a small ovenproof dish, covered with foil, until piping hot.

Shopper's tip
For a quick version, replace the vegetables and chopped tomatoes with 4 x 390g cans ratatouille.

Preparation time	**15 minutes**
Cooking time	**40 minutes**
Calories per portion	**594 Kcal**
Fat per portion	**21g**
of which saturated	**9g**
Serves	**4**
Suitable for freezing	

Ratatouille and ham pasta bake

Aubergine 1
Salt and freshly ground black pepper
Pasta shapes 300g (11oz)
Olive oil 2 tbsp
Onion 1, peeled and chopped
Red pepper 1, deseeded and chopped
Courgette 1, trimmed and chopped

Chopped tomatoes with garlic 2 x 400g cans
Dried mixed herbs 1 tsp
Cooked lean ham 225g (8oz), diced
Mozzarella 175g (6oz), grated
Grated Parmesan cheese 4 tbsp

Trim the aubergine and cut into small pieces. Layer in a colander or large sieve, sprinkling with salt. Set aside to drain for 30 minutes, then rinse well in cold water and pat dry.

Meanwhile, bring a large saucepan of water to the boil and cook the pasta according to the packet's instructions. Drain well and set aside.

While the pasta is cooking, heat the oil in a large saucepan and gently fry the onion and pepper for 5 minutes until just softened. Add the aubergine and courgette, and cook, stirring, for a further 5 minutes. Add the chopped tomatoes, herbs, ham and black pepper and stir. Bring to the boil, then reduce the heat, cover and leave to simmer for 15 minutes until the vegetables are tender.

Preheat the grill to hot. Stir the pasta and 110g (4oz) of the mozzarella into the vegetables. Pile into a large shallow ovenproof dish and sprinkle with the remaining mozzarella and the Parmesan cheese. Place under the grill and cook for 4–5 minutes until the cheese has melted and is bubbling. Serve immediately or cool and freeze, as described opposite.

Preparation time	**10 minutes**
Standing time	**30 minutes**
Cooking time	**25–30 minutes**
Calories per portion	**367 Kcal**
Fat per portion	**17g**
of which saturated	**6.1g**
Serves	**4**
Suitable for freezing	

Deep-pan bacon, cabbage and apple pancake

For the batter
Plain flour 125g (4½oz)
Salt a pinch
Egg 1
Whole milk 300ml (½ pint)

For the filling
Olive oil 1 tbsp
Unsmoked streaky bacon 8 rashers, de-rinded and chopped
Granny Smith apples 2, cored, peeled and thinly sliced
White cabbage ½ small, cored and shredded
Leek 1 small, trimmed, washed and shredded

1 First make the batter. Combine the flour and salt in a bowl, make a well in the centre and add the egg. Add half of the milk and gradually work into the flour using a whisk. Beat until smooth.

2 Gradually add the remaining milk, whisking all the time. Beat until the ingredients are well combined, then cover and leave in a cool place for 30 minutes. Stir the batter before using. Preheat the grill to medium.

3 Heat the oil in a large frying pan with an ovenproof handle and stir-fry the bacon for 2 minutes. Add the apple, cabbage and leek and cook, stirring, for a further 5 minutes until just tender. Pour the batter into the pan and cook over a low heat for about 15 minutes until set and then finish off under the grill until golden and puffy around the edges.

4 Serve immediately, cut into wedges, or cool and freeze as described in the Cook's tip below.

Cook's tip
Open freeze the wedges on a board lined with greaseproof paper, then wrap and seal. Defrost overnight in the fridge. Reheat slices on a baking sheet, covered in foil, until piping hot.

Shopper's tip
Look out for mini varieties of cabbage, useful for smaller portion cooking.

Preparation time	30 minutes
Cooking time	2½ hours
Calories per portion	737 Kcal
Fat per portion	44g
of which saturated	17.6g
Serves	4
Suitable for freezing	

Beef casserole with pastry toppers

Heat a flameproof casserole, add the pancetta and dry-fry for 5 minutes. Add the shallots and cook for 5 minutes. Stir the carrots, celery and garlic into the dish, cover and cook for 5 minutes to soften a little.

Preheat the oven to 160°C/325°F/Gas 3. Season the flour and toss the meat in it. Spoon the vegetables out of the casserole and into a bowl. If using frozen pastry for the pastry toppers, remove from the freezer now as it will take about 2 hours to thaw.

Heat the oil in the casserole and cook the floured meat, in batches if necessary. Add the red wine, stock, ketchup, herbs and reserved vegetables. Bring to the boil, cover and cook in the oven for 2 hours.

About 30 minutes before the end of cooking, heat the butter in a frying pan, add the mushrooms and cook until softened. Stir into the casserole, check the seasoning and liquid content and cook for 30 minutes.

Unroll the pastry and use a 9cm (3½in) round cutter to make four rounds. Place on a baking sheet and prick all over. Take the casserole out of the oven, turn up to 200°C/400°F/Gas 6. Brush the pastry with milk and sprinkle with paprika. Bake for 14–15 minutes until golden. Serve each pastry circle on a bowl of casserole.

Pancetta cubes 70g pack
Shallots 8, peeled and left whole
Carrots 2, peeled and sliced
Celery 2 sticks, chopped
Garlic 1 clove, peeled and chopped
Salt and freshly ground black pepper
Plain flour 1 tbsp
Braising steak 450g (1lb), cut into 2.5cm (1in) cubes
Olive oil 1 tbsp
Red wine 150ml (¼ pint)

Hot beef stock 300ml (½ pint)
Tomato ketchup 1 tbsp
Bay leaf 1
Rosemary 1 sprig
Thyme few sprigs
Butter 15g (½oz)
Cup mushrooms 110g (4oz), wiped and sliced

For the pastry toppers
Ready-rolled puff pastry 375g pack
Milk about 1 tsp
Paprika for sprinkling

Cook's tip
To freeze, cool the casserole and spoon into a container. Use within 3 months. Thaw in the fridge overnight. Reheat until hot.

Shopper's tip
If you can't find cubed pancetta, chop up four rashers of streaky bacon instead.

Preparation time	15 minutes
Cooking time	55 minutes
Calories per portion	299 Kcal
Fat per portion	14g
of which saturated	5.2g
Serves	4

Suitable for freezing

Beefy pesto peppers

Lean minced beef 350g (12oz)
Onion 1, peeled and finely chopped
Garlic 1 clove, peeled and crushed
Tomato purée 1 tbsp
Plain flour 1 tbsp
Beef stock 300ml (½ pint)

Salt and freshly ground black pepper
Green beans 150g (5oz), topped, tailed and cut in half
Red peppers 4
Pesto sauce 4 tbsp

Preheat the oven to 200°C/400°F/Gas 6. Put the minced beef in a medium-sized saucepan with the onion and garlic and heat gently, stirring, for about 5 minutes, until the meat browns all over.

Add the tomato purée and plain flour. Gradually stir most of the stock into the pan, bring to the boil and simmer for about 15 minutes, stirring occasionally, until thick and tender. Season and set aside.

Meanwhile, bring a small saucepan of water to the boil and cook the green beans for 4–5 minutes until just tender. Drain well and stir into the beef mixture.

Slit the peppers from tip to stem. Remove the seeds and core and fill each with the beef and bean mixture. Stand in a baking tin, pour the remaining stock around the peppers and top the meat in each pepper with a tablespoonful of the pesto sauce.

Bake in the oven for about 30 minutes until tender. Serve immediately accompanied with a fresh salad, or allow to cool and freeze as described below.

Cook's tip
To freeze, cool, wrap individually in foil and freeze. Thaw overnight in the fridge. Cover with foil and bake as above.

Shopper's tip
Red, yellow or orange peppers have the sweetest flavour, but green ones work just as well.

Preparation time	15 minutes
Cooking time	25 minutes
Calories per portion	600 Kcal
Fat per portion	35g
of which saturated	14.1g
Serves	4

Suitable for vegetarians + freezing

Pear and cinnamon crumble

Packham pears 4, peeled, cored and roughly chopped
Caster sugar 1 tbsp

For the crumble topping
Butter 100g (3½oz)
Demerara sugar 100g (3½oz)
Ground almonds 100g (3½oz)
Plain flour 100g (3½oz)
Ground cinnamon 1 tsp
Flaked almonds 2 tbsp

Preheat the oven to 190ºC/375ºF/Gas 5. Put the pears, sugar and 2 tablespoons of water in a medium-sized saucepan and cook gently for 5–8 minutes until the pears are softened – the exact time will depend on the ripeness of the pears. Using a slotted spoon, place the pears into four small dishes suitable for oven and freezer (ramekins are ideal for this).

Meanwhile, tip all the crumble topping ingredients, except the flaked almonds, into a food processor and press the pulse button several times until the mixture looks like fine breadcrumbs. Sprinkle the crumble over the pears and scatter with the almonds.

Bake in the oven for about 20 minutes or until the topping is golden. Serve immediately or freeze as described below.

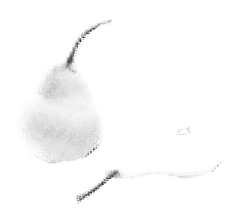

Cook's tip
To freeze, top the cool filling with the crumble and freeze for up to 1 month. Thaw in the fridge overnight and cook as above.

Shopper's tip
Buy pears in season and, if you can't find Packham, try Comice instead.

Preparation time	5 minutes
Freezing time	4–6 hours
Calories per portion	312 Kcal
Fat per portion	24g
of which saturated	20g
Serves	4

Suitable for vegetarians + freezing

Coconut ice cream

Coconut cream 250ml carton
Caster sugar 50g (2oz)
Ready-made custard 150g carton
Slices of mango to serve, optional

1. Tip the coconut cream into a bowl, whisk the caster sugar into the cream, then whisk the custard into the mixture. Pour into a suitable freeze-proof container and freeze until it's semi-frozen – 2-2½ hours. Alternatively, mix together the ingredients and then freeze in an ice cream machine.

2. If freezing in the deep freeze, once semi-frozen, stir the mixture well to break down any ice crystals, and then freeze until it's solid – 2-4 hours, stirring again once more just before it's completely set.

3. Remove from the freezer about 10 minutes before serving to allow the ice cream to soften slightly before scooping it out into individual bowls. Accompany with slices of mango, if using.

Cook's tip
To speed up the freezing of the ice cream, chill both the coconut cream and custard before you use them.

Shopper's tip
The coconut cream is UHT and comes in cartons, often found alongside the ingredients for Thai cooking.

Preparation time	10 minutes
Freezing time	2 hours
Calories per portion	329 Kcal
Fat per portion	15g
of which saturated	9.8g
Serves	4

Suitable for vegetarians + freezing

Fresh raspberry swirl ice cream

Luxury vanilla ice cream 1 litre tub
Raspberries 2 x 150g punnet, plus etxra
to serve, optional
Icing sugar 3 tbsp or to taste, sifted

Remove the ice cream from the freezer to
soften, while making the coulis.

To make the raspberry coulis, tip the fruit
into a food processor with the icing sugar
and whiz until smooth. Taste the raspberry
sauce and if it's too tart, add a little more
sugar, bearing in mind that the vanilla ice
cream is sweetened, too.

Tip the softened ice cream into a
freezerproof dish and mash it to soften.
Using a large spoon, swirl the raspberry
sauce through the ice cream and refreeze
for at least 2 hours before eating. Serve with
fresh raspberries.

Cook's tip
Serve the ice cream with a
scoop of summer berries
scattered over the top of
each bowl.

Shopper's tip
It is much easier buying food
and using the whole punnet or
container, there is no wastage and
it saves time weighing things out!

Preparation time	**20 minutes**
Cooking time	**30 minutes**
Calories per portion	**695 Kcal**
Fat per portion	**44g**
of which saturated	**16.3g**
Serves	**4**

Suitable for vegetarians + freezing

Peach and vanilla tartes tatin

Butter 25g (1oz)
Vanilla pod 1, split in half
Peaches 4, halved, stoned and sliced
Demerara sugar 1 tbsp
Ready-to-roll sweet pastry 500g pack

Heat the butter in a frying pan until sizzling. Add the vanilla pod, peaches and sugar and cook gently for 5 minutes or until the peaches are tender, stirring frequently. Remove the pan from the heat remove and reserve the vanilla pod and tip the peach mixture into two 18cm (7in) diameter gratin dishes (or shallow foil pie plates). Cover and leave to cool.

Preheat the oven to 200°C/400°F/Gas 6. Remove the pastry from the fridge 10–15 minutes before you want to use it (or according to pack's instructions).

Roll out half of the pastry onto a piece of non-stick baking paper (don't make it too thin or the pastry will break when you lift it up). Invert the pastry on to the fruit and peel off the paper. Chill while repeating with the second pie.

Bake in the oven for 20 minutes or until the pastry is crisp and golden. Turn out onto individual plates so the pastry becomes the base. Serve, or freeze as described in the Cook's tip.

Cook's tip
To freeze (for up to 1 month), cover the pie(s) with cling film. Thaw in the fridge overnight and bake in the oven as described.

Shopper's tip
Allow peaches to ripen for a few days in your fruit bowl before using them in this recipe; if too hard they have little flavour.

Preparation time	30 minutes
Cooking time	45 minutes
Calories per tartlet	727 Kcal
Fat per tartlet	34g
of which saturated	20.1g
Makes	4 tartlets

Suitable for vegetarians + freezing

Apple and blackberry tartlets

For the filling

Bramley cooking apples 500g (1lb 2oz), peeled, cored and sliced
Caster sugar 150g (5oz)
Lemon 1, finely pared zest and juice
Blackberries 150g (5oz), hulled

For the pastry

Plain flour 250g (9oz)
Salt a pinch
Butter 150g (5oz)
Caster sugar 1½ tbsp, plus extra for sifting
Egg 1 large, beaten with 2 tbsp water

To make the filling, put the apples in a saucepan, add the sugar, lemon zest and juice and 2 tablespoons of cold water. Cover the pan and cook gently until the apples are softened. Remove from the heat, add the blackberries and set aside to cool.

To make the pastry, sift the flour and a pinch of salt into a bowl. Add the butter and rub it into the flour until the mixture resembles fine breadcrumbs, then add the sugar. Finally, add the egg and mix to make a soft dough.

Knead the dough on a lightly floured surface and roll it out to 3mm (⅛in) thick. Using a 12.5cm (5in) diameter cutter, cut out four rounds from the pastry and set aside.

Preheat the oven to 220°C/425°F/Gas 7. Line a four-hole Yorkshire pudding tray with the pastry rounds and fill with the apple and blackberry mixture. Bring the pastry sides in and over the filling.

Cover the tartlets loosely with foil and bake in the oven for 35–40 minutes, until golden brown, removing the foil after 20 minutes. Sift a little caster sugar over the tartlets and serve.

Cook's tip
Open freeze at the end of step 4, then individually wrap in foil and freeze for up to 9 months. Thaw in the fridge overnight and then cook as described.

Shopper's tip
Bramley cooking apples are best for this recipe. Choose those that are unblemished.

Preparation time	**15 minutes**
Cooking time	**15–20 minutes**
Calories per portion	**310 Kcal**
Fat per portion	**0g**
of which saturated	**0g**
Serves	**4**

Suitable for vegetarians + freezing

Tipsy fruits

White wine 400ml (14fl oz)
Brandy 3 tbsp, optional
Caster sugar 110g (4oz)
Lemon 1 large, finely pared zest and juice
Peaches 2, quartered and stoned

Dessert apples 2 large, peeled, cored and thickly sliced
Apricots 4, halved and stoned
Pears 2, peeled, halved and cored

Pour the wine into a wide, shallow stainless steel saucepan (to prevent tainting the flavour or colouring of the fruit), add the brandy, sugar, lemon zest and juice and bring slowly to the boil – stirring occasionally.

Add the prepared fruit and cook gently for 15–20 minutes, or until just softened, carefully turning halfway through cooking to ensure they cook evenly. Take care not to over-cook the fruit, as it continues to cook after the pan is removed from the heat.

Allow the fruit to cool in the syrup until completely cold and then serve.

Cook's tip
To freeze, transfer the cooled fruit and syrup into plastic containers. Store for up to 1 year. Thaw in the fridge overnight – serve as above.

Shopper's tip
Select fruits that are just ripe as perfectly ripe ones may break up during cooking.

Preparation time	**20 minutes**
Cooking time	**40–50 minutes**
Calories per portion	**493 Kcal**
Fat per portion	**26g**
of which saturated	**15.3g**
Serves	**4**

Suitable for vegetarians + freezing

Tangy fruit puddings

For the toppings

Orange 1
Maraschino or glacé cherries 25g
(1oz), quartered
Sultanas 25g (1oz)

For the sponge

Butter 110g (4oz), softened to room
temperature
Caster sugar 110g (4oz)
Eggs 2 large, at room temperature
Self-raising flour 110g (4oz)

Custard to serve, optional

Grease four 175ml (6fl oz) individual pudding moulds, and then line the bottom of each one with a small round of greaseproof paper.

Using a sharp, stainless steel knife, cut away the peel and white pith from the orange. Then, cutting between the white connective tissue, and holding the orange over a small bowl, remove the segments. Roughly chop the segments and add them to the orange juice. Add the cherries and sultanas, and mix. Divide between the two moulds.

To make the sponge mixture, beat together the butter and sugar until very light and creamy. Gradually beat the eggs into the mixture and then gently fold in the flour. Divide the sponge mixture between the moulds.

Cover each pudding basin with foil and then steam the puddings for 40–50 minutes until well risen and the tops spring back when pressed. Cook in a tiered steamer or in a saucepan filled with boiling water to halfway up the side of each mould. When cooked, serve immediately with custard or allow to cool and freeze as described below.

Cook's tip
Allow the puddings to cool, cover with foil, then freeze for up to 9 months. Steam from frozen as in step 5.

Shopper's tip
For alternative toppings, use 45g (1½oz) chopped dark chocolate with 1 tbsp double cream, or 2 tbsp golden syrup or marmalade.

Preparation time	5 minutes
Cooking time	1¼ hours
Calories per portion	748 Kcal
Fat per portion	53g
of which saturated	28g
Serves	4

Suitable for vegetarians + freezing

Bread and butter pudding

Lightly butter a medium-sized freezer and ovenproof dish. Then spread the butter over one side of each of the slices of bread, and cut each slice into four triangles. Arrange the slices, butter-side up, in the dish. Scatter with the raisins or sultanas, lifting some of the pieces of bread slightly so the fruit goes under them.

Lightly whisk together the cream, milk, eggs, sugar and spice and pour over the bread. If freezing (see Cook's tip, below), tightly cover the dish with cling film.

To cook, preheat the oven to 160°C/325°F/ Gas 3. Bake in the centre of the oven for 1–1¼ hours, or until it is light golden and feels firm when lightly pressed in the centre. Take care not to cook for too long or the custard will curdle. Serve immediately, as it will sink down once it is out of the oven.

Butter 25–50g (1–2oz), softened
Sliced white bread 8 slices, crusts removed
Raisins or sultanas 3–4 tbsp

Double cream 284ml carton
Milk 300ml (½ pint)
Eggs 4
Caster sugar 4 tbsp
Ground mixed spice 2 tsp

Cook's tip
To freeze, prepare to end of step 2 and freeze for up to 1 month. Thaw in the fridge overnight, remove cling film and bake.

Shopper's tip
If you don't want to buy a whole loaf of bread, you can slice 2–3 brioche rolls and use these instead.

Cook's tip
To freeze, make the slice up to the end of step 3. Wrap in cling film and freeze for up to 1 month. Thaw in the fridge overnight, remove the cling film and bake as in step 4.

Shopper's tip
If you can't find a small pack of marzipan, use half a 454g or 500g pack and wrap the rest well so it doesn't dry out.

Preparation time	**10 minutes**
Cooking time	**30 minutes**
Calories per portion	**701 Kcal**
Fat per portion	**32g**
of which saturated	**9.9g**
Serves	**4**

Suitable for vegetarians + freezing

Peach and marzipan slice

Ready-rolled chilled puff pastry 375g
pack
Marzipan 270g pack
Sliced peaches 411g can, drained
Egg 1, beaten
Smooth apricot jam or glaze 3 tbsp

Lightly butter a baking sheet. Unroll the pastry and cut it lengthways into two, having one side slightly wider than the other. If necessary, trim the length of the pieces of pastry so they will fit on the baking sheet and then transfer the smaller piece onto the baking sheet.

Roll out the marzipan so it's 1.5cm (¾in) narrower and shorter than the base piece of pastry. Brush water on the edges of the narrow piece of pastry and place the marzipan on top. Arrange the peach slices down the centre.

Lightly fold the wider piece of pastry in half and cut through the pastry where it's folded into lines about 2cm (¾in) apart. Open out the pastry and place over the peaches. Press the edges of the pastry well to seal them and to ensure that the marzipan won't leak out. Trim the edges.

To cook, preheat the oven to 220°C/425°F/Gas 7. Brush the top of the slice with egg glaze and then bake for 30–35 minutes until it's risen and golden in colour. Remove it from the oven and transfer it to a wire rack.

Melt the jam with 1 tablespoon of water, either in a bowl in a microwave oven or in a small saucepan on the hob. Brush
the glaze over the hot pastry.
Serve hot or cold.

Sweet sensations

Few people catering for a small family or just for themselves have the inclination to create delicious desserts.

However, when you see how simple and scrumptious these puddings are you'll be very tempted to give them a try.

Ponder the delights of hot toffee banana custard, baked pears with maple syrup or raspberry and lemon meringue nests. These are almost more trouble to eat than to cook: they are all quick, easy and fresh ways to finish off supper. Go on; give in to your temptation!

Preparation time	5 minutes
Cooking time	10 minutes
Calories per portion	595 Kcal
Fat per portion	51g
of which saturated	29g
Serves	1
Suitable for vegetarians	

Naughty chocolate mousse

Dark chocolate 40g (1½oz), chopped
Double cream 5 tbsp
Very strong black coffee 1tbsp
Soft light brown sugar 1 tsp or to taste
Chocolate-filled wafers to serve, optional

Slowly melt the chocolate in a heatproof bowl set over a pan of gently simmering water. Remove from the heat and stir with the double cream, coffee and sugar to taste.

Pour into a coffee cup and chill for 20 minutes or until the chocolate mixture has a mousse texture. Serve with chocolate-filled wafers.

Cook's tip
If you don't like the taste of coffee, just leave it out of the method. The result will be even more chocolatey.

Shopper's tip
Check the cocoa content (it should be about 70 per cent) and make sure that the only fat it contains is cocoa butter.

Preparation time	**5 minutes**
Cooking time	**5 minutes**
Calories per portion	**445 Kcal**
Fat per portion	**22g**
of which saturated	**13.6g**
Serves	**1**
Suitable for vegetarians	

Hot toffee banana custard

Butter 15g (½oz)
Light brown sugar 1 tbsp
Banana 1, peeled and sliced
Ground cinnamon ½ tsp

Ready-made custard 150g carton
Slice of ginger cake to serve, optional

1 Melt the butter in a small frying pan over a medium heat and add the sugar. Stir until it has dissolved.

2 Add the sliced banana and cinnamon, and cook, stirring, for 2–3 minutes until just beginning to soften. Stir the custard into the pan, heat for a further minute and serve immediately on a slice of ginger cake.

Cook's tip
You can serve this as a chilled pudding by allowing the banana to cool before stirring it into cold custard.

Solo shopper's tip
Individual cartons of custard are good store cupboard standbys. They keep for several weeks unopened.

Preparation time	5 minutes
Standing time	10 minutes
Calories per portion	499 Kcal
Fat per portion	18g
of which saturated	6.5g
Serves	1
Suitable for vegetarians	

Blueberry sponge sundae

Blueberry muffin 1
Blueberries 50g (2oz)
Virtually fat-free vanilla yogurt 200g carton
Dark chocolate 15g (½oz), grated

Remove the muffin from its paper case and cut into small cubes. Place in the bottom of a serving glass with most of the blueberries. Top with the yogurt.

Stand for 10 minutes to allow the sponge to soften, then sprinkle with the remaining blueberries and the grated chocolate and serve immediately.

Cook's tip
To freeze berries. Wash, pat dry and lay in a single layer on a tray. Freeze until solid and then pack into freezer bags or containers.

Shopper's tip
For an alternative flavour combination, try using a dark chocolate muffin and fresh raspberries.

163

Preparation time	**10 minutes**
Cooking time	**5 minutes**
Calories per portion	**854 Kcal**
Fat per portion	**59g**
of which saturated	**27.1g**
Serves	**2**
Suitable for vegetarians	

Ice cream with hot chocolate sauce

Dark chocolate 110g (4oz), broken into small pieces
Single cream 150ml (5fl oz)
Brandy 1–2 tbsp
Freshly squeezed orange juice 6 tbsp
Vanilla ice cream 6 scoops

Raspberry or strawberry conserve 2 rounded tsp, optional
Pecan nuts 50g (2oz), roughly chopped
Cherries and halved strawberries to decorate
Fan wafers to serve, optional

Put the chocolate, cream, brandy and orange juice into a small saucepan and stir over a medium heat until the chocolate melts and is smoothly blended, taking care not to overheat the sauce – it should be hot, but not boiling.

Put a scoop of ice cream into the bottom of two tall chilled sundae glasses or large wine glasses and then add the raspberry or strawberry conserve.

Add one or two more scoops of ice cream and then add half of the hot chocolate sauce. Top with the remaining ice cream and chocolate sauce, then sprinkle with pecans and decorate with cherries and strawberries. Add the fan wafers and serve.

Cook's tip
Alternatively, arrange scoops of ice cream in the centre of large, individual plates and pour the chocolate sauce around.

Shopper's tip
For the very best flavour, buy a good quality organic ice cream that is additive free and does not contain vegetable fat.

165

Preparation time	10 minutes
Cooking time	5 minutes
Calories per portion	537 Kcal
Fat per portion	34g
of which saturated	17.5g
Serves	2
Suitable for vegetarians	

Vanilla ice cream with bitter orange

Butter 50g (2oz)
Caster sugar 4 tbsp
Water 2 tbsp

Orange 1, juice only
Chunky marmalade 2 tbsp
Vanilla ice cream 2–4 scoops

1 To make the sauce, melt the butter in a small saucepan and add the sugar and water. Stir until the sugar dissolves, then boil the mixture without stirring, until it caramelises.

2 Remove the pan from the heat and add the orange juice and marmalade. Stir until the marmalade melts, then return the pan to the heat and simmer the sauce for 1–2 minutes. Remove the pan from the heat once more and leave the sauce to cool.

3 Place the scoops of ice cream into serving dishes and spoon the sauce over the top. Serve immediately.

Cook's tip
The sauce is quite rich, so if you don't want to serve it all, it will keep in a covered dish in the fridge for up to 1 week.

Shopper's tip
For the best flavour, choose a good-quality vanilla ice cream that is made from natural vanilla.

Preparation time	5 minutes
Cooking time	5 minutes
Calories per portion	278 Kcal
Fat per portion	20g
of which saturated	12.3g
Serves	2
Suitable for vegetarians	

Ruby fruits with white chocolate sauce

Mixed frozen berries 200g (7oz)
Crème fraîche 4 tbsp
White chocolate 50g (2oz), broken into small pieces
White chocolate curls to decorate

Divide the frozen berries between two shallow dishes and leave to thaw a little while you make the sauce.

Put the crème fraîche and broken chocolate into a small saucepan and heat gently, stirring until the chocolate melts. Whisk gently until smooth but don't overheat, otherwise the sauce will separate.

Pour the hot sauce over the berries so they start to soften and the sauce sets on the fruit. Serve immediately, decorated with the white chocolate curls.

Cook's tip
To make chocolate curls, run a swivel bladed peeler over the underside of a block of white chocolate.

Shopper's tip
A tub of crème fraîche keeps for a week in the fridge. Use it to make a quick sauce for pasta with some pesto sauce.

Preparation time	5 minutes
Cooking time	3 minutes
Calories per portion	264 Kcal
Fat per portion	13g
of which saturated	1.2g
Serves	2
Suitable for vegetarians	

Baked pears with maple syrup

Pears 2
Dried cranberries or cherries 2 tbsp
Maple syrup 2 tbsp

Ground cinnamon a pinch, optional
Pecan nuts 6 halves, roughly broken
Natural yogurt or crème fraîche to serve

Peel and halve the pears, keeping the stalks on if you like. Scoop out the cores with a melon baller or teaspoon. Put the halves, cut-side down, in a shallow dish. Sprinkle with the dried fruit and add 1 tablespoon of the maple syrup. Sprinkle with a little cinnamon, if using.

Cover the dish with a microwave lid or cling film and cook on high power for 3 minutes, checking and stirring the dried fruit after 2 minutes. To bake in the oven, preheat it to 180°C/350°F/Gas 4, cover the dish with foil and bake for 15–20 minutes.

Serve the pears with a little more maple syrup drizzled over and sprinkled with the broken nuts. Add a generous spoonful of thick yogurt or crème fraîche and serve.

Cook's tip
If you halve the recipe, just cook for 1½ –2 minutes in the microwave or the pears will be overcooked and tasteless.

Shopper's tip
Buy dried cranberries or cherries in small packs; they also add colour and flavour to your cereal, cakes and puddings.

Preparation time	**5 minutes**
Calories per portion	**317 Kcal**
Fat per portion	**21g**
of which saturated	**12.9g**
Serves	**2**
Suitable for vegetarians	

Raspberry and lemon meringue nests

Meringue nests 2
Crème fraîche ½ x 200ml carton
Lemon curd 2–3 tbsp

Raspberries 150g (5oz) carton
Icing sugar for dusting
Mint leaves to decorate

Place the meringues on serving plates. Mix together the crème fraîche, lemon curd and half of the raspberries, taking care not to over-mix it or it will go runny. Divide the mixture between the meringue nests.

Arrange the remaining raspberries next to the nests and dust with a little icing sugar before serving decorated with mint leaves.

Cook's tip
The remaining crème fraîche may be stirred into some pasta with grated cheese for a very quick cheese sauce.

Shopper's tip
Choose a good quality luxury lemon curd for a natural flavour filling; some cheaper curds can have a slightly artificial taste.

Bakes and cakes

Baking can be so satisfying and therapeutic, but many people who live alone or in a couple find it isn't worth the bother, as often their creations go dry before they have been eaten.

These baking recipes, however, are created specifically with the small household in mind. They can either be made in smaller quantities, or they have a longer shelf-life in the cupboard or freezer.

So you don't have to wait for the next church fête before you don your apron – try out some of these scrumptious cakes today and enjoy a delicious snack with your morning cuppa.

Preparation time	15 minutes
Cooking time	20–25 minutes
Calories per muffin	216 Kcal
Fat per muffin	13g
of which saturated	7.6g
Makes	9 muffins

Suitable for vegetarians + freezing

Raspberry muffins

Self-raising flour 200g (7oz)
Baking powder 1 tsp
Caster sugar 75g (3oz)
Egg 1, beaten
Milk 175ml (6fl oz)
Butter 125g (4½oz), melted and cooled
Fresh raspberries 175g (6oz)

1. Preheat the oven to 190ºC/375ºF/Gas 5. Line a muffins tin with 9 muffin cases. Sift the self-raising flour, baking powder and caster sugar into a mixing bowl.

2. Whisk the beaten egg with the milk and cooled butter and stir into the dry ingredients, until just mixed (don't overmix). Then add the raspberries.

3. Divide the mixture between the muffin cases and bake in the oven for 20–25 minutes until risen and lightly golden. Enjoy one while still warm! Then leave the rest to cool on a wire rack.

Cook's tip
If you have raspberries left over from your punnet, stir them into Greek yogurt and top with runny honey for a quick and tasty pud.

Shopper's tip
If raspberries aren't around, these muffins are just as scrummy if you use the same weight of fresh blueberries instead.

Preparation time	10 minutes
Cooking time	35 minutes
Calories per muffin	303 Kcal
Fat per muffin	11g
of which saturated	6g
Makes	4 muffins

Suitable for vegetarians + freezing

Muesli and cranberry muffins

Self-raising flour 110g (4oz)
Mixed spice ½ tsp
Salt a pinch
Caster sugar 50g (2oz)
Unsweetened muesli 40g (1½oz)
Egg 1, beaten
Butter 40g (1½oz), melted
Whole milk 2 tbsp
Cranberry sauce 4 tbsp

Preheat the oven to 190°C/375°F/Gas 5. Line a deep cup muffin tin with 4 paper muffin cases. Sift the flour, spice and salt into a mixing bowl. Add the sugar and muesli, reserving some muesli for sprinkling.

Make a well in the centre and gradually blend in the egg, melted butter and milk to form a thick batter. Fold the cranberry sauce into the batter.

Divide the mixture between the muffin cases (they should be quite full), sprinkle over the remaining muesli and bake in the oven for 30–35 minutes until risen and lightly golden. Transfer to a wire rack to cool. Serve warm split with butter and jam.

Cook's tip
Serve these muffins for breakfast or tea – they are best eaten on the day they are baked. They freeze well.

Shopper's tip
For an alternative, replace the cranberry sauce with ready made apple sauce, and use a mixture of oats and sultanas instead of the muesli.

Preparation time	10 minutes
Cooking time	15 minutes
Calories per cookie	146 Kcal
Fat per cookie	4g
of which saturated	2.3g
Makes	10 cookies
Suitable for vegetarians	

Chocolate meringue cookies

Egg whites 2
Icing sugar 110g (4oz)
Water biscuits 110g (4oz), finely crushed
Dark chocolate 100g bar, melted
Vanilla extract a few drops

1   Preheat the oven to 180°C/350°/Gas 4 and line a baking sheet with greaseproof paper. Whisk the egg whites until stiff and then continue whisking while gradually adding the icing sugar. Fold the biscuit crumbs, melted chocolate and vanilla into the whites.

2   Place dessertspoonfuls of the mixture onto the lined baking sheet, flattening them slightly. Bake in the centre of the oven for 12–15 minutes or until firm to touch.

Cook's tip
To crush the water biscuits, whizz them in a food processor until finely ground, or place in a plastic bag and crush with a rolling pin.

Shopper's tip
Water biscuits usually come in a 200g pack, so if you want to use the whole pack, double the recipe.

Preparation time	**10 minutes**
Freezing time	**2 hours**
Cooking time	**12 minutes**
Calories per cookie	**269 Kcal**
Fat per cookie	**13g**
of which saturated	**8g**
Makes	**10 cookies**

Suitable for vegetarians + freezing

Freezer cookies

Plain flour 200g (7oz)
Baking powder 1 tsp
Butter 150g (5oz), cubed
Caster sugar 200g (7oz)
Egg 1
Vanilla extract a few drops

1 Sift the flour and baking powder into a bowl and add the butter. Rub in the butter until the mixture resembles fine breadcrumbs. Add the caster sugar, egg and vanilla extract and mix together to form a dough. Alternatively, place all the ingredients into the bowl of a food processor and whizz until a dough is formed.

2 Shape the dough into a log about 20cm (8in) long and wrap in greaseproof paper. Wrap in a plastic bag, seal and freeze for at least 2 hours, or for up to 1 month.

3 Preheat the oven to 200°C/400°F/Gas 6. Line a baking sheet with greaseproof paper. Remove the dough from the freezer and use a knife with a long sharp blade to cut the dough into 10 slices each about 1cm (½in) thick. Lay the slices, spaced well apart, on the baking sheet.

4 Bake the cookies in the centre of the oven for 10–12 minutes, or until light golden in colour. Remove the baking sheet from the oven and leave the cookies to cool for a few minutes, then transfer them to a wire rack to cool completely.

Cook's tip
As the cookie dough is stored in the freezer (for up to 1 month), you can slice off as many cookies as you want at a time.

Shopper's tip
Vanilla extract has a better flavour than vanilla essence as it is made from the real thing.

Preparation time	20 minutes
Cooking time	1–1¼ hours
Calories per slice	281 Kcal
Fat per slice	10g
of which saturated	5.5g
Makes	8 slices

Suitable for vegetarians + freezing

Banana cake

Plain wholemeal flour 200g (7oz)
Baking powder 2 heaped tsp
Very ripe bananas 450g (1lb), peeled
Butter 75g (3oz), softened
Golden caster sugar 110g (4oz)
Eggs 2 large, beaten

Preheat the oven to 180°C/350°F/Gas 4. Grease and line a deep 18cm (7in) diameter cake tin. Sieve together the flour and baking powder returning any bran from the sieve to the bowl. Blend the bananas in a food processor until smooth.

In a separate large bowl, cream together the butter and sugar until pale and fluffy, then gradually add the eggs and beat until smooth. Beat the banana purée into the mixture. Fold in the flour and pour into the prepared baking tin.

Bake for 60–75 minutes or until a skewer inserted into the middle comes out clean. Turn out and cool on a wire rack. Cut the cake into portions. Wrap each slice in cling film and pop in the freezer. To use, reheat each slice in the microwave on high for about 60 seconds. The exact time will depend on the wattage on your microwave and the thickness of the portion – be careful, the cake is hot when it comes out of the microwave.

Cook's tip
This cake recipe is a great way of using up leftover very ripe bananas.

Shopper's tip
Overly ripe bananas are often sold at a reduced price, so snap them up for this recipe.

Preparation time	**30–40 minutes**
Cooking time	**45–55 minutes**
Calories per slice	**245 Kcal**
Fat per slice	**11g**
of which saturated	**6.3g**
Makes	**20 slices**

Suitable for vegetarians + freezing

Fruited ginger slab cake

Butter 225g (8oz), at room temperature
Soft dark brown sugar 225g (8oz)
Black treacle 2 tbsp
Eggs 4 large, beaten
Self-raising flour 350g (12oz)
Ground ginger 1–1½ tbsp
Orange 1 large, grated zest and 4 tbsp juice

Stem ginger 50g (2oz), roughly chopped
Syrup from ginger 2 tbsp
Dark glacé cherries 50g (2oz), halved or quartered
Raisins 50g (2oz)
Mixed peel 50g (2oz)
Sultanas 50g (2oz)

Preheat the oven to 180°C/350°F/Gas 4. Grease the base and sides of a baking dish or small roasting tin, measuring approximately 30 x 25 x 6cm (12 x10 x 2½in) deep and then line with non-stick baking paper.

In a large bowl, beat together the butter and sugar until very light and fluffy. Add the black treacle, and then gradually beat the eggs into the mixture. Sift the flour and ginger into the bowl and mix gently. Then add the rest of the ingredients and mix gently.

Spoon the cake mixture into the prepared dish or tin and spread evenly. Bake the cake in the centre of the oven for 45–55 minutes, or until it feels firm to the touch, and a skewer, when inserted in the centre, comes out clean.

Allow the cake to cool in the baking dish or tin, then very carefully turn it out onto a board. Cut in half lengthways, then cut each half into 10 thick slices. Wrap individually in cling film, or in twos or fours, as preferred. Stored in a large plastic container or cake tin the cake will keep well for at least one week. Alternatively, freeze the individually wrapped slices, thawing them out as required.

Cook's tip
This deliciously moist ginger cake improves in flavour if kept for 2–3 days before eating – however, it can be sampled as soon as it is cold!

Shopper's tip
Although slightly more expensive, organic flours give excellent results for baking cakes and biscuits.

Preparation time	45–50 minutes
Cooking time	15–20 minutes
Calories per tartlet	372 Kcal
Fat per tartlet	20g
of which saturated	7.7g
Makes	6 tartlets
Suitable for vegetarians + freezing	

Cherry and almond tartlets

For the pastry
Plain flour 150g (5oz)
Icing sugar 25g (1oz)
Unsalted butter 75g (3oz), cut into small cubes
Egg yolks 2 large

For the filling
Egg whites 2 large
Caster sugar 75g (3oz)
Ground almonds 50g (2oz)
Chopped hazelnuts 25g (1oz)
Vanilla extract ½ tsp
Fresh or canned black cherries 24, stoned and halved
Icing sugar for sifting

1 To make the pastry, sift the flour and icing sugar into a bowl, add the butter and rub into the flour until the mixture resembles breadcrumbs. Add the egg yolks and mix together, to make a soft, but not sticky, dough.

2 Knead the dough on a lightly floured surface and then roll out to about 3mm (⅛in) thick. Using a 12.5cm (5in) plain round cutter, cut out six rounds from the pastry (rekneading and rerolling the trimmings as necessary). Line individual 8.5cm (3½in) fluted tartlet tins with the pastry rounds, press firmly into the flutes and then trim off the excess. Chill while making the filling.

3 Preheat the oven to 200°C/400°F/Gas 6. To make the filling, put the egg whites, caster sugar, ground almonds, chopped hazelnuts and vanilla into a small bowl and mix together.

4 Spoon the almond and hazelnut mixture into the lined tins and spread it evenly. Then arrange the cherries in a circle, cut-sides down, on top.

5 Place the tins on a baking tray and cook the tarts for 15–20 minutes, or until the filling is lightly browned and firm to the touch. Serve warm or cold, sifted with icing sugar.

Cook's tip
You can make smaller individual tartlets in bun tins or, for a large version, use a 20cm (8in) fluted flan tin instead.

Shopper's tip
Look for cherries that are unblemished, large and succulent. If black cherries are unavailable, use large red ones.

Preparation time	**10 minutes**
Cooking time	**25–30 minutes**
Calories per square	**145 Kcal**
Fat per square	**7g**
of which saturated	**4.1g**
Makes	**16 squares**
Suitable for vegetarians + freezing	

Fruity chocolate squares

Butter 110g (4oz), at room temperature
Caster sugar 110g (4oz)
Self-raising flour 150g (5oz)
Eggs 2
Milk 2 tbsp
Dried ready-to-eat apricots 75g (3oz), snipped into small pieces
Red cherries (dried or glacé) 50g (2oz), snipped into small pieces
Plain chocolate chips 25g (1oz)

Cook's tip
The recipe for this cake can be varied depending on which dried fruits you have in your cupboard.

Shopper's tip
Buy dried fruit when it's on special offer as it does keep for a few months if you ensure the bag is sealed well.

Preheat the oven to 180°C/350°F/Gas 4 and line a 17.5cm (7in) square cake tin with non-stick baking paper.

In a large bowl, cream the butter with the sugar until light and fluffy, then add the flour, eggs and milk and mix until smooth. Stir the chopped fruit into the mixture and then spoon into the tin and smooth the top. Sprinkle with the chocolate chips and lightly press them into the mixture.

Bake for 25–30 minutes until risen and firm. Cool for 10 minutes, take out of the tin, cool on a wire rack and cut into squares.

Preparation time	**10 minutes**
Cooking time	**35 minutes**
Calories per slice	**136 Kcal**
Fat per slice	**6g**
of which saturated	**2.9g**
Makes	**10 slices**

Suitable for vegetarians + freezing

Frosty top lemon loaf

For the cake
Butter 50g (2oz), at room temperature
Caster sugar 75g (3oz)
Self-raising flour 75g (3oz)
Ground almonds 25g (1oz)
Egg 1
Lemon ½, grated zest only

For the topping
Lemon ½, juice only
Granulated sugar 50g (2oz)

1. Preheat the oven to 180°C/350°F/Gas 4, then strip line and grease a 450g (1lb) loaf tin with non-stick baking paper.

2. In a large bowl, mix together all the cake ingredients until smoothly blended. Spread the mixture in the tin and bake for 35 minutes until just firm to the touch.

3. For the topping, mix the lemon juice with the sugar and spoon it evenly over the cake as soon as it comes out of the oven.
Leave in the tin to cool for at least 10 minutes then turn out onto a wire rack to cool. Slice for serving.

Cook's tip
Leave out the lemon zest and topping but add 50g (2oz) dried fruit to the mixture and sprinkle the top with 25g (1oz) chopped hazelnuts before baking.

Shopper's tip
It's handy to have two small loaf tins to cook two cakes at once.

Preparation time	**10 minutes**
Cooking time	**20 minutes**
Calories per crescent	**190 Kcal**
Fat per crescent	**13g**
of which saturated	**6.1g**
Makes	**16 crescents**

Suitable for vegetarians + freezing

Almond crescents

Plain flour 250g (9oz)
Unsalted butter 175g (6oz)
Icing sugar 50g (2oz), plus extra for dredging
Egg yolk 1
Milk 1 tbsp
Ground almonds 100g pack

Preheat the oven to 180°C/350°F/Gas 4. Tip all the ingredients into the bowl of a food processor, and whiz until they start to bind together into a dough, but take care not to over-process the dough. Alternatively, tip the flour into a bowl and add the butter, cut into pieces, and then rub the butter into the flour until the mixture resembles fine breadcrumbs. Add the remaining ingredients and continue to rub together all the ingredients to form a dough.

Divide the dough into 16 portions and roll each piece into a smooth ball without cracks. Then pat each into a crescent shape about 1cm (½in) thick. Place the crescents on a lightly buttered baking sheet. Bake in the centre of the oven for 15–20 minutes or until they are a pale golden colour.

Sift a thick layer of icing sugar onto a plate. While the biscuits are still hot, slide a palette knife under each one in turn to transfer to the plate of sifted icing sugar in a single layer. Dredge a layer of icing sugar over the top of the biscuits, then leave them to cool.

Cook's tip
For a spicy variation, add some grated orange zest and ground cinnamon, and substitute orange juice for the milk.

Shopper's tip
Unsalted butter gives the best flavour, but salted butter can be used, too.

Index

Previous books

Dairy Cookbooks are widely recognised as some of the most reliable recipe books ever written. With over 30 million copies sold, almost every household will have used a Dairy Cookbook at some point.

The first book – The Dairy Book of Home Cookery – was published in 1968 and has been revised and reprinted several times due to its unprecedented popularity.

In recent years, five new cookbooks have been published – The New Dairy Cookbook, the Quick & Easy Dairy Cookbook, the Year Round Dairy Cookbook, Around Britain Dairy Cookbook and Hearty & Healthy.

The Dairy Book of Home Cookery

(416 pages) was last published in 1992, and contains hundreds of recipes, from how to make the perfect cheese sauce to creating an impressive soufflé. Now in its third reprint!

The New Dairy Cookbook

(192 pages) was published in 2001 and features 150 delicious new recipes for all occasions.

Quick & Easy Dairy Cookbook

(192 pages) was published in 2003 and has 130 tasty recipes, which can be prepared in less than 30 minutes.

Year Round Dairy Cookbook

(192 pages), published in 2005 and features 130 seasonal recipes to give the taste buds a treat the whole year round.

Around Britain Dairy Cookbook

(192 pages) was published in 2006 and contains favourite regional recipes plus new ones with a contemporary twist.

Hearty & Healthy

(192 pages) was published in 2007 and contains recipes to help you eat well, keep well and enjoy good food.

How to order

For pricing and ordering details please ring:

08450 948128   calls charged at local rate

There is more information on our website:

www.dairydiary.co.uk